3-D LONDON

THE ULTIMATE PICTORIAL STREET ATLAS AND GUIDE

CHELSEA
REACH

CHEYNE WALK

BATTERSEA BRIDGE

3-D LONDON
THE ULTIMATE PICTORIAL STREET ATLAS AND GUIDE

Written by Fiona Duncan, Leonie Glass and
Caroline Sharpe

Maps created by Irwin Technical

First published 1990 by
Robert Nicholson Publications
16 Golden Square, London W1R 4BN

Nicholson is an imprint of Bartholomew – the Cartographic Division of the
Collins Publishing Group

London Transport Underground Map: registered user no 90/1056

Conceived, edited and designed by
Duncan Petersen Publishing Ltd,
5, Botts Mews, Chepstow Road,
London W2 5AG

Filmset by SA Composing, Rayleigh, Essex
Printed and bound in Hong Kong by Regent Publishing Services Ltd

ISBN 0 948576 43 X

Every reasonable care has been taken to ensure the information in this
guide is accurate, but the publishers and copyright holders can accept no
responsibility for the consequences of errors in the text or on the maps,
especially those arising from closures, or those topographical changes
occurring after completion of the aerial survey on which the maps are based.

ACKNOWLEDGEMENTS

The authors would like to thank the many people who have helped them with their research. Dozens of people gave information about buildings they live or work in; the London Tourist Board & Convention Bureau and the City of London Information Centre gave invaluable help; and of the many publications consulted in the course of writing, the authors particularly acknowledge:

The London Encyclopaedia, ed. Ben Weinreb and Christopher Hibbert (Macmillan); *In London* (Nicholson Publications); *The American Express Pocket Guide to London* (Mitchell Beazley); *Economist Business Traveller's Guides: London* (Collins); *Geoffrey Fletcher's London*, Geoffrey Fletcher (Penguin); *The Streets of London*, S. Fairfield (Papermac); *The Buildings of England, London: The Cities of London and Westminster*, Bridget Cherry and Nikolaus Pevsner; *Guide to The Architecture of London*, Edward Jones (Weidenfeld); *London Statues*, Arthur Byron (Constable); *The Blue Plaque Guide to London* (Journeyman Press); *Louise Nicholson's Definitive Guide to London*, Louise Nicholson (The Bodley Head); *The Blue Guide to London*, ed. Ylva French (A & C Black); *London Pub Guide* (Nicholson Publications); *Companion Guide to London*, David Piper (Collins); *A Wanderer in London*, E. V. Lucas (Methuen); *Naked City*, David Brazil (Queen Anne Press); *London, 2000 Years of a City and its People*, Felix Barker and Peter Jackson (Papermac); *Chelsea Seen from its Earliest Days*, John Bignell; (Hale); *The City of London*, James Bartholomew (Herbert Press); *The Markets of London*, Alec Forshaw and Theo Bergstrom (Penguin); *Wren's London*, Colin Amery (Lennard Publishing); *Nairn's London*, Ian Nairn (Penguin); *London Museums and Collections* (CP Guidebooks); *London's Riverside: From Hampton Court in the West to Greenwich Palace in the East*, Suzanne Ebel and Doreen Impey (Luscombe); *Michelin Tourist Guide to London* (Michelin). *400 Glorious Pubs*, John Thirkell (Imprint).

Finally, we would especially like to thank Anja Kutscher for painstakingly double-checking our facts by tramping the streets of London.

Editorial

Editor   Fiona Duncan
Assistant editor   Laura Harper
Index   Rosemary Dawe

Design
Art director Mel Petersen
Designers Chris Foley and Beverley Stewart

Aerial survey by Aerofilms Ltd, Boreham Wood, Hertfordshire
Maps created by Irwin Technical Ltd, 10-18, Clifton Street, London EC2A 4BT

Contents

Acknowledgements	5
About this book	8-9
Master location maps	10-21
Essential information for visitors to London	22-35
London Underground map	36-37
London bus routes	38-39
THE ISOMETRIC MAPS	40-155
Index of points of interest described in text	156-165
Index of people of interest described in text	165-169
Index of street names	169-176

About this book

How the mapping was made

Isometric mapping is produced from aerial photographic surveys. One was specially commissioned for *London: A New Dimension:* the helicopter flew at about 1,500 feet, with the camera angled at 45°. Weather conditions had to be slightly overcast in order to achieve maximum detail on the buildings.

Scores of enlargements were made from the negatives, which Irwin Technical, a group of technical illustrators in London (address on page 176), then used to create the maps. A team of seven, working in pen and ink, took well over 1,000 hours to complete the task.

'Isometric' projection means that verticals are the same height, whether in the foreground or the background – at the 'front' (bottom) of the page or at the 'back' (top). Thus the diminishing effect of perspective is avoided and all the buildings, whether near or distant, are shown in similar detail and appear at an appropriate height.

The order of the maps

The map squares are arranged in sequence running from north to south and from west to east. For further details, see the master location maps on pages 8-21.

Numerals on maps

Each numeral on a map cross refers to the text printed down the right hand border of the map. The numbers generally read from the top left of each map to the bottom right, in a west-east direction. However, there are deviations from this pattern when several interesting features occur close together, or within one street.

Opening and closing times

If a museum, display or exhibition is open during regular working hours, opening and closing times are not mentioned in the text accompanying the maps. Brief details are however given when opening times are irregular. In the case of historic or otherwise interesting buildings, assume that you cannot gain access to the interior unless opening times are mentioned.

Prices

£   means one person can eat for less than £10.
££   means one person can eat for less than £20.
£££ means one person generally pays more than £20.
Wine is not included.

Coverage

No guide book can cover everything of interest in London. This one contains a particularly wide range of information, and the writers concentrated on aspects of the city brought out by the special nature of the mapping, with emphasis on historical or general information that helped explain the fabric, evolution and working of the city. They have also tended to draw attention to the outstanding, even the peculiar, sometimes at the expense of the obvious and well-established, in the belief that this best reveals the essential character of a city. There is, in addition, much about eating, drinking, shopping and other practical matters.

Master location maps

14–15

20–21

12–13

18–19

16–17

Master location maps

Master location maps

Master location maps

Master location maps

Master location maps

Master location maps

Transport

From airports to city

Heathrow is served by underground (tube), buses and taxis.

The London Underground's Piccadilly Line (connected to airport terminals by a moving walkway) takes passengers direct from its Heathrow stations (separate stops for terminal 4 and for terminals 1, 2 and 3) to central London, whence you can transfer to any other tube line (see map on pages 36-37). It operates between 5 am (6.45 on Sun) and 11.30 pm.

If you have more luggage than you can comfortably manage on the tube, a bus may be preferable. London Transport operates its Airbus services A1 and A2 between 6.20 am and 10.20 pm to Victoria or Euston Stations, calling at various central London points on the way.

Taxis are plentiful, though they are an expensive alternative, costing not less than £20 to central London. Ignore cab drivers touting for work inside the terminals; always go to an official rank.

For car drivers, central London is approached on the M4 motorway, and the drive usually takes about 30 minutes, though it can take much longer depending on the traffic (worst during rush-hour). When driving to Heathrow, you should leave the motorway at junction 3 for the new terminal 4 (signposted), and junction 4 for terminals 1, 2 and 3.

Gatwick is near Crawley in Surrey, some 25 miles from central London, about one hour by car along the M23 motorway. There is an excellent train service, the Gatwick Express, between the airport and Victoria Station, running every 15 minutes during the day and evening, and hourly throughout the night. The 777 Green Line bus service runs approximately every hour between 4.20 am and 10 pm to Victoria Coach Station and takes about 1½ hours.

If you intend to leave your car at Heathrow or Gatwick for more than a short time, remember to leave time to park it in one of the long-term car parks (a bus service to the airport is provided). Short-term car parks are close to the terminals but also very expensive.

London buses

'Just hop on a bus' may seem rather a daunting epithet to first-time visitors to London, faced with the complex route system. In reality, the system is fairly straightforward, and cheaper and more fun than the tube, though much slower. Red double-decker buses, each displaying a number, run along correspondingly numbered routes; check which route you want from the chart on pages 38-39. Their timing can be somewhat erratic (timetables displayed at bus stops should not be relied on), and they are notorious for always appearing in groups of three after a long interval. Bus stops display the numbers of the buses which call there. If the stop has the word 'request', the bus will only halt if a passenger on the bus rings the bell, or someone at the stop raises their hand. The conductor (or, on some buses, the driver) will collect your fare; the amount varies depending on how far you are travelling. Buses run from about 5 am to 11.30 pm, with night buses on selected routes. All major night bus routes pass through Trafalgar Square.

Some buses stop short of the end of their route; look at the front of the bus as it approaches to see where it is destined to stop, and check that it is far enough for you; other people in the queue will usually help.

In addition to the traditional double-decker buses, London Transport has recently introduced small single-decker buses called hoppers. These operate on central London routes, for example between South Kensington and Waterloo (No. C1), and are designed for people who want to travel only a couple of stops or so.

The London Underground

London's tube stations are by and large depressing, even squalid. They could well do with an expensive overhaul to bring them up to the standards of, say, the Paris Metro. Trains are often overcrowded, especially at rush-hours. The Underground network, however, is extensive and the system efficient, and it is a fast way of getting about the city. Each station is on at least one of nine Underground lines. These are featured by the map on page 36, printed in black and white (whereas tube maps displayed on the Underground itself are in colour, with a different colour to identify each line). In central London particularly, a station may be served by several lines, and this makes it easy to change from one line to another. To trace your route, and where you should, if necessary, change trains, simply follow the lines from the station from which you depart to your destination. Trains run daily from around 5.30 am (7.30 am on Sunday) to around midnight.

Stations are identified at street level by the London Transport symbol of a red circle cut by a blue horizontal line. Tickets can be bought at machines or, if you are in doubt, from the ticket office, where you should state your destination. Keep your ticket until it is collected at the end of your journey.

For details of both bus and tube routes, timetables and fares (including various special tickets and flat-rate passes) you can telephone 222 1234. London Transport have Travel Information Centres at Victoria, St James's Park, Oxford Circus, Piccadilly Circus, Euston, King's Cross and Heathrow tube stations. Free tube and bus maps are available from any Underground ticket office.

Taxis

Londoners who find themselves in foreign cities such as New York are usually terrified by the indigenous taxi drivers, who appear to have scant regard either for traffic regulations or for human life. By contrast, London cabbies are superb drivers, and neither they nor their famous stately black taxis are given to flashy manoeuvres. They also know their way about town and have had to pass an exam on the subject, known as 'the knowledge'. If you are not at a taxi rank (outside stations, large stores and so on) you can hail a taxi in the street, if its yellow 'For Hire' sign is illuminated above the windscreen. The fare is shown on the meter. You should add a 10-15 per cent tip, though to save time, cabbies prefer it if you simply round up the fare and say "Keep the change". Under £5 add approximately 50p, over £5 add about £1. Sometimes the drivers can be difficult about taking their 'fares' to destinations to which they don't want to go; remember that they are obliged to take you if the destination is within six miles of the pick-up point. If you wish to order a taxi by phone, there are several numbers to call including Computer Cab (286 0286), Radio Taxis (272 0272) and Dial-a-Cab (253 5000). If you leave something behind in a taxi, try calling in at the taxi lost property office at 15 Penton Street, N1.

The phrase 'black cab' to denote a licensed taxi with a meter is becoming confusing, since licensed cabbies are starting to drive a new make of taxi called Metrocab which, apart from looking different, appears in several different colours. The much-loved black cab may soon be a thing of the past.

Unlicensed taxis are not to be recommended unless you know a reputable company. They are usually ordinary saloon cars (often scruffy) and are referred to as minicabs. They are frequently unreliable, and finding your destination may prove a problem. As minicabs don't have meters, the fare must be agreed on at the start of the trip.

Private Cars

Driving is becoming increasingly problematic in London: traffic is slow moving on most main roads, and blockages can often occur in side streets. For newcomers, the street layout is confusing and complicated. Courtesy amongst drivers is not unknown; certainly, they are not as aggressive as in Rome, Paris or Madrid.

Apart from remembering to drive on the left and obeying traffic regulations (laid out in the Highway Code, available from HMSO Bookshop, 49 High Holborn, WC1. There are three rules of which you should be particularly aware: **1** Don't drink and drive. More than about three glasses of wine, or their equivalent, will send you over the limit on the breathalyser which police carry for on-the-spot checks on suspicious motorists. **2** Wear seat belts. Police can impose fines if they see drivers and front-seat passengers without their seat belts fastened. **3** Don't park illegally. Parking on single or, more dangerously, double yellow lines can, and frequently does, result in a traffic warden giving you a parking ticket for which you have to pay a fine, or in your car being clamped or towed away. The latter two evils involve much inconvenience, several hours of your time and well in excess of £60 of your money. Better to endeavour to find an empty parking meter (difficult in central London; don't let the meter run into 'excess time' or again you may be fined) or park in an NCP car park. To find one, follow the blue 'parking' signs.

Visiting Britain

By train London's main British Rail stations ring the city, and link the capital with all major towns in Britain through the fast Inter-City service, as well as Motorail and sleeper trains. The main stations are Paddington (information tel. 262 6767), serving south-west England and south Wales; Charing Cross, Waterloo and Victoria (tel. 928 5100), serving the south and south-east; Liverpool Street (tel. 283 7171), serving Cambridge and East Anglia; Euston and St Pancras (tel. 387 7070), serving the Midlands, North Wales, the north-west and west Scotland; King's Cross (tel. 278 2477), serving the north-east and east Scotland.

In addition to the Underground, London's suburbs are served by British Rail's Network SouthEast service. Journeys further afield are made on the main line network, departing from London's British Rail main line stations.

By air British Airways (tel. 897 4000 for flight times and reservations) and British Midland (tel. 589 5599) offer 'shuttle' services between Heathrow and Manchester, Edinburgh, Glasgow and Belfast airports. As well as these two main operators, several other companies offer scheduled flights to Britain's 30 or so regional airports. For details, contact a travel agent, such as Thomas Cook (1 Marble Arch, W1; tel. 402 9424, and many other branches).

London City Airport, situated in Docklands on the east of the city, and opened in 1987, is a 'stolport' (short take off/landing), mainly suited to businessmen. For information on which British and European cities are currently served, tel. 474 5555.

By coach National Express is the largest coach company in Britain. Victoria Coach Station is the London terminus for their services to al parts of the country. It is a slow, but inexpensive way of travelling. For details of services and fares tel. 730 0202.

By car Britain's toll-free motorway network is extensive, reaching most parts of the country, and where 'A' (major) and 'B' (secondary) roads may provide the shortest route, the motorway is usually quicker. The speed limit on motorways and dual carriageways is 70 mph (110 kmph), 60 mph (100 kmph) on single carriageways and 30 mph (50 kmph) in built-up areas. Be warned that many motorways, most notoriously the M1, are plagued by 'cone disease', with long sections subjected to contra-flow systems, marked by a series of orange cones, caused by road-works. Long delays can occur at these places. Motorways from all directions converge on London, now all linked by the M25 motorway which rings the city. An inner ring is formed by the A205 South Circular and A406 North Circular. Approaching London, once off the motorway, the driver is plunged bewilderingly into the suburbs. If in doubt, for central London, follow signs for the 'West End'.

For further information on travelling in Britain, you can visit the British Travel Centre, 4-12 Lower Regent Street, SW1; tel. 730 3400.

Useful data

Tourist information

London Tourist Board information centres are located at:

■ Victoria Station forecourt, SW1; open daily summer 9 am-10.30 pm, winter 9 am-7 pm (5 pm on Sun).

■ Harrods, Knightsbridge, SW1 (4th floor); open during store hours.

■ Selfridges, Oxford Street, W1 (basement services arcade); open during store hours.

■ Tower of London, West Gate, EC3; open summer only, daily 10 am to 6 pm.

■ Heathrow, terminals 1, 2 and 3, Underground Station concourse, Heathrow Airport; open daily, 9 am-6 pm.

■ Heathrow, terminal 2, Arrivals concourse, Heathrow Airport; open daily 9 am-7 pm.

Telephone information, including daily events, can be obtained by dialling 730 3488 between 9 am and 6 pm.

For children's events, call Kidsline on 222 8070 between 4 and 6 pm in term time, and 9 am and 4 pm in holidays.

Disabled visitors can receive guidance from the Disabled Information Service run by RADAR (Royal Association for Disability and Rehabilitation) on 637 5400.

Sightseeing tours

London Transport's double-decker Round London Sightseeing Tour bus departs every half hour daily, except bank holidays, from Piccadilly Circus, Marble Arch, Baker Street and Victoria Street. Tickets can be bought on the bus, but they are cheaper if purchased from any London Transport or London Tourist Board information centre (cut-price, direct-entry tickets to Madame Tussauds also included). Circular tour lasts 1½ hours; buses are open-topped in summer: tel. 227 3456. Cityrama tours also depart every 30 minutes daily, except Christmas Day, from Trafalgar Square, Piccadilly Circus, Lower Regent Street, Westminster Abbey and Grosvenor Gardens, and provide eight-language taped commentaries: tel. 720 6663. Most luxurious is the Harrods half- or full-day tour, also with an eight-language commentary: tel. 581 3603.

Apart from Harrods, various other companies offer luxury coach tours, with stop-offs for guided visits round London's principal sights, or for river-boat cruises:

■ Evan Evans, 27 Cockspur Street, SW1; tel. 730 3477.
■ Frames Rickards, 11 Herbrand Street, WC1; tel. 837 3111.
■ Golden Tours, 132 Cromwell Road, SW7; tel. 743 3300.

All can be booked through the London Tourist Board Centres at Victoria, Harrods or Selfridges.

River trips Boats run frequently every day from Westminster and Charing Cross piers to the Tower and Greenwich, and in summer further downstream to the Thames Barrier and upstream to Kew or Hampton Court. For further information, fares and departure times, contact the recorded River Boat Information Service, tel. 730 4812; also Thames Line Riverbus Service, tel 987 0311.

Walking tours The following companies organize morning or afternoon theme walks in various parts of London:
■ Discovering London; tel. (0277) 213704.
■ London Walks; tel. 441 8906.
■ Citisights of London; tel. 739 2372.
■ Cockney Walks; tel. 504 9159.

Private guided tours For a guide plus car call either Take a Guide; tel. 221 5475, or British Tours; tel. 629 5267.

Shopping, banking and business hours

Generally speaking, shops in central London are open between 9 or 9.30 am and 5 to 6 pm, Mon-Sat. Fashion and gift shops may not open until 10 am. Some specialist shops are closed on Sat, or open only in the mornings. Outside the city centre, some shops close between 1 and 2 pm for lunch and for one afternoon a week, usually on Wed or Thur. In central London most shops stay open one evening a week for 'late-night' shopping. Oxford Street shops stay open until 8 pm on Thur, and Knightsbridge and King's Road shops stay open until 7 pm on Wed. Certain chains of food stores have very late opening hours, as well as some small corner shops. Giant supermarkets such as Sainsbury's and Safeway stay open at least until 8 pm; and on some nights as late as 10 pm.

On Sunday, some newsagents are open in the mornings, also the occasional grocery store or delicatessen.

Banks are open from 9.30 am to 3.30 pm, Mon-Fri. A few bank branches open on Saturday. In central London they are: Barclays at 140-142 King's Road, SW3, 74 Kensington High Street, W8 and also at 28 Hampstead High Street, NW3 – all open 9.30 am-12 noon; National Westminster at 466 Oxford Street, W1 and 250 Regent Street, W1, open 9.30 am-12.30 pm; and Lloyds at 399 Oxford Street, W1 and at Selfridges, Oxford Street, W1 between 10 am-3 pm and 9 am and 5 pm respectively.

Bureaux de change (poorer exchange rates than banks) have longer opening hours, and can be found at airports and stations, as well as in some Underground stations and main shopping streets.

There are several 24-hour bureaux de change, for example Chequepoint at Marble Arch, Earl's Court Road and Queensway.

'Nine to five' are the normal working hours for office workers, although many stay longer and City workers are particularly early risers. The 'rush-hour' occurs between about 8 and 9.30 am and 5 and 7 pm, Mon-Fri.

Public holidays

It feels like a Sunday, with banks and shops closed, on the following days of the year: New Year's Day (1 January), Good Friday, Easter Monday, May Day (first Mon in May), Spring Bank Holiday (last Mon in May), August Bank Holiday (last Mon in August), Christmas Day (25 December), Boxing Day (26 December).

The post

Main post offices are open from 9 am to 5.30 pm, Mon-Fri, and 9 am to 1 pm on Sat. The post office in William IV Street, off Trafalgar Square, is an exception, open from 8 am to 8 pm Mon-Sat and from 10 am to 5 pm on Sun. The opening hours of sub post offices vary; they often form part of newsagents or corner stores. Parcels should be taken to post offices for weighing; various special postal services – such as Recorded Delivery and Red Star – are available. Stamps are bought at post offices, and letters are posted in the red pillar-boxes that dot the streets, or in less conspicuous wall-mounted post-boxes. Sending mail by first-class post is recommended, since it is faster, more reliable and only a few pence dearer than second class.

New Scotland Yard

Telephones

The old-style red telephone boxes have almost entirely been replaced by new black and yellow ones (also silver and blue or silver and green). All have clear instructions on how to use them and can be found on streets, in stations, large shops, public buildings and pubs. Some take coins, others take 'Phonecards' which can be bought in post offices and shops displaying the Phonecard sign.

The dialling code for London until 6 May 1990 is 01. You only need to use this prefix if you are calling from outside London. After 6 May 1990 the prefix changes: 071 for central London numbers; 081 for greater London numbers. These prefixes are added to the existing numbers whether dialling from outside London, or from greater to central London or vice versa. Most numbers in this guide have 071 prefixes.

Some call boxes contain the local – in this case London – telephone directories, with information about codes and operator services printed in the front of the A-K book. Here are some useful numbers:

■ For help from an operator dial 100.

■ For the international operator dial 155.

■ For directory enquiries dial 142 or 192.

■ For international directory enquiries dial 153.

■ To send a Telemessage within the UK or to the USA dial 190.

■ For international telegrams dial 193.

■ For the speaking clock dial 123.

■ For the Weatherline (south-east England weather forecast) dial 246 8091.

■ In an emergency, dial 999 for the police, ambulance and fire services. The call is free; you will be asked which service you require.

Publications

The weekly magazines *Time Out* and *City Limits* have comprehensive listings of entertainments and events, including pop and classical concerts. The *Evening Standard*, a daily evening paper, contains details of theatres and cinemas, and *The Times* and *The Independent* have good information.

The travel sections of book shops will reveal a wide range of guidebooks to London. For the disabled, Nicholson publishes *Access in London*, and a useful and inexpensive guide for children, *Children's London*. Good general bookshops include Hatchards at 187 Piccadilly, W1 and Waterstones at 121 Charing Cross Road, WC2 and other branches (open until 7.30 pm Mon-Fri, 7 pm on Sat). The Pan Bookshop, 158 Fulham Road, SW10 is open till 10 pm Mon-Sat, 9 pm on Sun.

For your nearest public library, see under 'Libraries' in the telephone directory. The largest are: Westminster Central Reference Library, St Martin's Street, WC2, tel. 828 8070; and the Guildhall Library, Aldermanbury, EC2, tel. 606 3030.

Foreign embassies

Embassies, high commissions and consulates are listed in the telephone directory under 'Embassy', 'High Commissioner' and 'Consuls' or under the country's name. Here is a selection:

- **Australia** Australia House, Strand, WC2; tel. 379 4334.
- **Canada** 1 Grosvenor Street; W1; tel. 629 9492.
- **France** 24 Rutland Gate, SW7; tel. 581 5292.
- **Germany (Federal Republic)** 23 Belgrave Square, SW1; tel. 235 5033.
- **Ireland** 17 Grosvenor Place, SW1; tel. 235 2171.
- **Italy** 14 Three Kings Yard, W1; tel. 629 8200.
- **Japan** 46 Grosvenor Street, W1; tel. 493 6030.
- **Netherlands** 38 Hyde Park Gate, SW7; tel. 584 5040.
- **New Zealand** 80 Haymarket, SW1; tel. 930 8422.
- **Spain** 20 Draycott Place, SW3; tel. 581 5921.
- **USA** 24 Grosvenor Square, W1; tel. 499 9000.

Medical information

Hospitals

The following hospitals are among those in London with 24-hour casualty departments: St Mary's, Praed Street, W2, tel. 755 6666; St Bartholomew's (Barts), West Smithfield, EC1, tel. 601 8888; Royal Free, Pond Street, NW3, tel. 794 0500; St Thomas', Lambeth Palace Road, SE1, tel. 928 9292; St Stephen's, Fulham Road, SW10, tel. 352 8161; Guy's, St Thomas Street, SE1, tel. 407 7600.

Late-night chemists

Chemists operate a duty rota for evenings and Sunday so that one chemist in each area will be open at these times; details in local papers. There are no 24-hour chemists in London, but Bliss Chemist, Willesden Lane, NW6, is open every day from 9 am to 2 am. Boots, Piccadilly, and some other central London branches are open until 8 pm Mon-Sat. Bliss Chemist, Marble Arch, is open 9 to midnight, Mon-Sun.

Doctors

Should you need to see a doctor, either (if your condition warrants it) for a home visit, or preferably at his or her surgery, consult the *Yellow Pages* telephone directory under the heading 'Doctors (Medical Practitioners)'. If you are an EEC resident, reciprocal health arrangements will make it easy for you to reclaim charges on your return, provided you have the necessary documentation before you travel. With non-EEC residents, the situation is more complex, and visitors are advised to consult health professionals at home before travelling. Full details are also given in the manual published by the Department of Health and Social Security entitled *NHS Treatment of Overseas Visitors*.

Dental treatment

A list of dentists will be found under 'Dental Surgeons' in the *Yellow Pages* telephone directory. For emergency treatment, you can go to Eastman Dental Hospital, 256 Gray's Inn Road, WC1, tel. 837 3646 (Mon-Fri, 9 am-4.30 pm); or to Guy's, St Thomas Street, SE1, tel. 407 7600 (daily 9 am-3.30 pm, Mon-Fri go to 23rd floor of the tower block, at weekends go to Casualty Department).

London Underground map

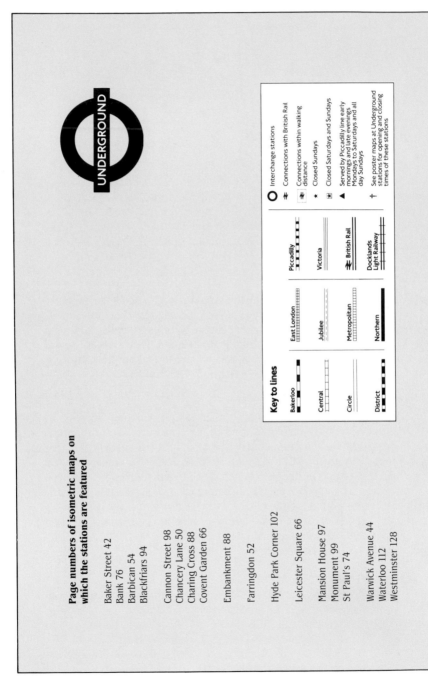

Page numbers of isometric maps on which the stations are featured

Baker Street 42
Bank 76
Barbican 54
Blackfriars 94

Cannon Street 98
Chancery Lane 50
Charing Cross 88
Covent Garden 66

Embankment 88

Farringdon 52

Hyde Park Corner 102

Leicester Square 66

Mansion House 97
Monument 99
St Paul's 74

Warwick Avenue 44
Waterloo 112
Westminster 128

UNDERGROUND

Key to lines

Bakerloo	Piccadilly
Central	Victoria
Circle	British Rail
District	Docklands Light Railway
East London	
Jubilee	
Metropolitan	
Northern	

○ Interchange stations

₦ Connections with British Rail

₦ Connections within walking distance

★ Closed Sundays

⊞ Closed Saturdays and Sundays

▲ Served by Piccadilly line early mornings and late evenings Mondays to Saturdays and all day Sundays

† See poster maps at Underground stations for opening and closing times of these stations

UNDERGROUND

37

London bus routes

	Aldwych	Angel	Baker Street	Bank	Chelsea/King's Road	Earl's Court	Elephant & Castle	Euston	Hammersmith	Hampstead	Highgate	High St Kensington	Holborn	Hyde Park Corner	Kew	King's Cross	Knightsbridge
Aldwych																	
Angel	4/171																
Baker Street	13	30															
Bank	6/11	43	6/13														
Chelsea/King's Road	11	22/38	22/30	11/22													
Earl's Court	30/9	74/38	30	74/25*	31												
Elephant & Castle	1/68	171	12/13	133	12/11	A											
Euston	68/77A	30/73	18/30	68/6	68/11	30	68										
Hammersmith	11	10/73	27	11	11	9/31	9/12	10									
Hampstead	24/15	24/30	24/30	24/6	24/22	24/30	24/1	24/73	24/10								
Highgate	134/176	43	134/30	43	134/22	134/30	134/1	134/73	134/10	210							
High St Kensington	9	10/73	27	9/6	31	31	9/12	10	9/10	73/10	10/134						
Holborn	68/77A	19/38	6/159	8/22B	22	22/30	68/77A	68/77A	8/1	7/24	8/134	19/134					
Hyde Park Corner	9	19/73	30/74	9/25	19/22	30/74	9/12	10/73	9/10	73/24	73/134	9/10	19/22				
Kew	27/9	27/73	27	K	27/31	27/31	B	27/10	27	27/24	27/134	27	C	27/10			
King's Cross	77A	30/73	18/30	77A/6	73/22	30	45/63	30/73	10	C11	73/134	10	77A	10/73	10/27		
Knightsbridge	9	19/30	30/74	9/6	19/22	30/74	9/12	10/30	9/10	10/24	10/134	9/52	19/22	14/30	10/27	10/30	
Liverpool Street	6/11	43+	6/159	6/8	11	25/30	35/133	6/68	11	8/24	22B/134	6/9	8/22B	9/11	D	6/77A	11/9
Ludgate Circus	6/15	4	15/13	6/11	11	9/30	45/68	6/68	11	15/24	17*	15/9	6/68	9/11	9/27	45/63	11/9
Marble Arch	6/15	30/73	30/74	6/8	16/22	74	12	10/73	10	73/24	73/134	10	7/8	16/73	10/27	30/73	30/74
Monument	15/501*	43	15/159	43/133	15/11	E	35/133	15/68	11	15/24	43	15/9	501*	15/9	E	15/77A	15/9
Notting Hill Gate	15/12	12/73	27	12/6	31	31	12	12/73	27	27/24	27/134	28/31	12/8	52	27	12/73	52
Olympia	9	10/73	27	9/6	9/31	73/31	9/12	10	10/27	10/24	10/134	9/10	73/8	9/10	27	10	9/10
Oxford Circus	6/15	73	13/159	6/8	73/22	73/30	12/53	10/73	10	73/24	73/134	10	7/8	10/73	10/27	10/73	10/137
Oxford St/Selfridges	6/15	73	13/159	6/8	73/22	74	12	10/73	10	73/24	73/134	10	7/8	10/73	10/27	10/73	10/137
Paddington	15	27/73	27	15/6	27/31	27/31	15/73	27/73	27	27/24	27/134	27	7	36/506*	27	27/36	36/30
Piccadilly Circus	6/9	19/38	13/159	6/15B*	19/22	9/30	12/53	14/14A	9	19/24	19/134	9	19/22	9/14	27	38/10	14/9
Richmond	27/9	27/73	27	K	27/31	27/31	B	27/10	27	27/24	27/134	27	C	27/10	27	27/10	27/10
St Paul's	6/15	4	15/13	6/11	11	25/30	141	6/68	11	15/24	17*	15/9	6/68	9/11	9/27	17*	11/9
Sloane Square	11	19	19/74	11	11/22	19/12	11/73	19	11	19/24	22/134	C1	19/22	19/137	E	19/30	19/137
South Kensington	14/9	30	30/74	14/25*	49/219	30/74	45	14/30	49/10	30/24	14/134	49/C1	14/19	14/30	49/27	30	14/49
Tate Gallery/Millbank	77A	88/73	2A/11	77A/22	36/22	36/30	510	77A	36/10	88/24	I	36/36	77A	2B/36	J	77A	36/14
Tottenham Court Rd	176	73	8/13	8/22B	19/22	73/30	176	10/73	10	24	134	10	7/8	14/73	10/27	10/73	14/19
Trafalgar Square	6/9	15/171A	13	6/11	11	9/30	12/53	77/77A	9	24	29/134	9	77A	9/27	77A	9/27	77A/9
Victoria	11	38/73	2A/2B	11/25*	11	36/30	510	73	11	24	73/134	73/C1	52/C1	25/38	36/73	52/27	73
Warren Street	176	30/73	27/30	29/8	73/22	30	29/12	10/73	10	24	134	10/27	29/10	10/73	10/27	10/73	10/30
Waterloo	68/171A	4/171A	68/73	76/501*	1/11	C1/31	1	68	68/9	1/24	176/134	C1	68/171	68/27	C1/27	68/77A	C1
Westminster	77/77A	29/73	159	11	11	C1/31	12/53	77/77A	11	24	29/134	C1	77/77A	12/9	C1/27	77A	C1

* Buses run Mon-Fri only. Some buses do not run on Sundays – check at bus stops

\+ From Liverpool St walk along Eldon St to Moorgate for direct bus service (43)

The following journeys are difficult by bus, involving two changes and the alternative tube connections are suggested:

A Bakerloo line to Embankment then change to District line
B District line to Embankment then change to Bakerloo line
C District line to Earls Court then change to Piccadilly line
D Circle line to South Kensington then change to District line
E District line direct
F Escalator link to Bank then change to Northern line
G District line to South Kensington then change to Circle line
H Circle or District lines direct
I Victoria line from Pimlico to Warren Street then change to Northern line
J Victoria line from Pimlico to Victoria then change to District line
K District line to Monument then use escalator link

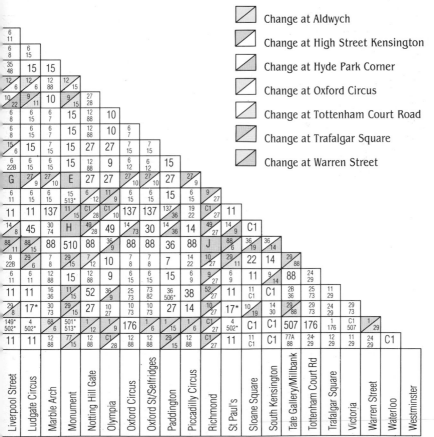

Change at Aldwych
Change at High Street Kensington
Change at Hyde Park Corner
Change at Oxford Circus
Change at Tottenham Court Road
Change at Trafalgar Square
Change at Warren Street

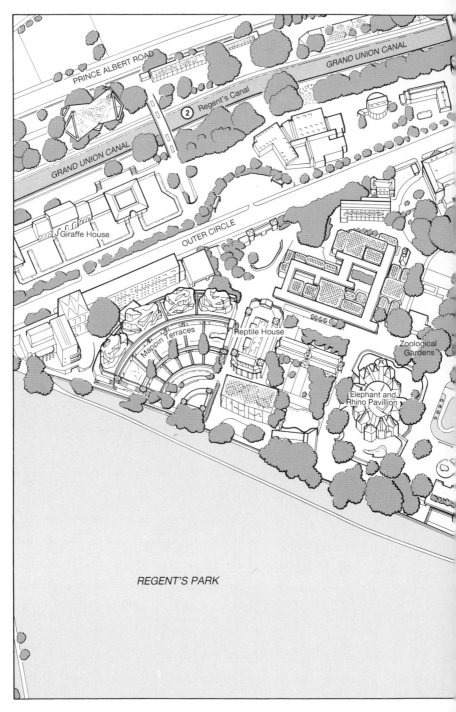

PRINCE ALBERT ROAD

GRAND UNION CANAL

② Regent's Canal

GRAND UNION CANAL

GRAND UNION CANAL

OUTER CIRCLE

Giraffe House

Mappin Terraces

Reptile House

Zoological Gardens

Elephant and Rhino Pavillion

REGENT'S PARK

London Zoo

① Colloquially known as London Zoo, the **Zoological Gardens** were laid out by Decimus Burton in 1827, over five acres, to display the Zoological Society of London's collection of animals, and opened to a curious public in 1847. There are now over 8,000 animals occupying 36 acres of Regent's Park. London Zoo has often been the first to house animals outside their natural habitat: in 1843 the world's first reptile house opened there; the keeper tried unsuccessfully to charm a cobra, only to be bitten and die. Through the Society, which was founded in 1826 by Sir Thomas Stamford Raffles, the Zoo has become a world centre for scientific research. Its architecture reflects the changing views of the Society on the way animals should be kept: the Giraffe House (1836) is one of the few early buildings to survive. The Mappin Terraces (closed for redevelopment) were revolutionary when designed in 1913 by Belcher and Joass, with the idea that animals should range more freely, their cages hidden from view. The Penguin Pool, designed by Lubetkin and Tecton, is described by Pevsner as a *tour de force* derived from Le Corbusier. Since 1959, various architects have contributed to the redevelopment, including Sir Hugh Casson (Elephant and Rhino Pavilion), and J.W. Toovey (the new Lion Terraces). The most famous of the Zoo's buildings is the tangled-looking aviary designed by Lord Snowdon and opened in 1965. In 1988, the Zoo's financial crisis was eased by a "one-off" government grant, and redevelopment plans are in progress; the threat of extinction, however, is far from assuaged. ② **Regent's Canal,** part of the Grand Union Canal linking London and Birmingham, bisects the Zoo and allows a romantic form of transport to and fro. You can dine aboard the motor launch *My Fair Lady*, which cruises from Camden to Little Venice and back each evening (tel. 485 4833). The canal was opened in style in 1820, with architect John Nash sailing down in the City State Barge and brass bands playing. ③ **Broad Walk,** a stately tree-lined promenade connecting the Outer Circle. In it is the Parsee drinking fountain, a heady mixture of Victorian Gothic and the East, topped by a bust of Queen Victoria, which was donated by Sir Cowasjee Jahangir.

CLARENCE TERRACE

OUTER CIRCLE

INNER CIRCLE

Cornwall Terrace

ALLSOP PLACE

BAKER STREET

MELCOMBE STREET

GLENTWORTH STREET

⊖ Baker Street

ALLSOP PLACE

YORK

MARYLEBONE ROAD

Marylebone Road/Regent's Park

① **Regent's Park** was once Henry VIII's hunting forest, and later its small-holdings provided London with hay and dairy produce. In 1811 the leases ran out, and the Crown seized the opportunity to develop the 500 acres of land. An architects' competition was launched and, thanks to the unswerving patronage of the Prince Regent, John Nash's brilliant design for a *rus in urbe* of majestic proportions won. His plan for two circles of terraces disguised as individual palaces, with 26 villas hidden in the landscaped parkland, was considerably modified, but Regent's Park remains a tribute to Nash's genius and foresight. Amongst its features are ② The **Boating Lake**, a focus for Sunday family life, with a band playing nearby; ③ **Queen Mary's Rose Gardens**, where intoxicating scents abound in summer, and the Open Air Theatre braves the weather to perform Shakespeare in a wonderfully atmospheric setting (two restaurants £); ④ **Clarence Terrace**, by Nash and Decimus Burton (Wilkie Collins lived at No. 2, later the home of Louis Macneice). ⑤ **Cornwall Terrace**, by Nash and Burton with, at No. 10, a glorious two-storey bow window decorated with caryatids, the British Academy at Nos 20-21; ⑥ **York Terrace**, designed by Nash as two separate terraces divided in the middle to allow a view of St Marylebone Church, with entrances at the back to preserve the illusion of two palaces. South of the park ⑦ the **Abbey National** tower block (1920s by J.J. Joass), incorporates 221B Baker Street, the fictional lodgings of Sherlock Holmes. ⑧ **The London Planetarium** takes you on a magical, if neck-aching, journey across the night sky; and the Laserium uses ingenious tricks to dance images across the dome. ⑨ Over-rated and plagued by queues, **Madame Tussauds** has drawn in the crowds to see the tableaux, the famous wax figures from past and present and the Chamber of Horrors for well over 150 years. ⑩ A church has stood on this site since 1400. The present name of **St Marylebone** derives from the days when the church was called St Mary-by-the-Bourne, referring to the River Tyburn which ran beside. Built by Thomas Hardwick in 1813, the church has an eye-catching cupola and a cold blue, white and gold interior. Amongst many other luminaries, Byron and the daughter of Nelson and Lady Hamilton were christened in the church, and Robert Browning married Elizabeth Barrett here.

Warwick Avenue
CLIFTON VILLAS
WARWICK AVENUE
RANDOLPH
WARWICK PLACE
BLOMFIELD ROAD
WARWICK AVENUE
DELAMERE TERRACE
BLOMFIELD VILLAS
WESTBOURNE TERRACE ROAD
LITTLE VENICE
WARWICK CRESCENT
HARROW ROAD
WESTWAY

Little Venice

① **Clifton Villas**, probably named in celebration of Brunel's Clifton Suspension Bridge (1894). ② **Clifton Nurseries** (No. 5), largest in central London, boasting a vast selection from azaleas to kumquats, as well as attractive antique garden ornaments. ③ **Warwick Castle** (6 Warwick Place), Regency pub, with panelled walls, open fire and prints of the early 20thC canal scenes, in the heart of Little Venice. ④ **Clifton Little Venice** (No. 3), specializes in architectural salvage. You might find anything here from an 18thC gazebo to a couple of Doric columns. ⑤ One of the oldest roads in the area, **Warwick Avenue** was laid out in the 1840s and lined with grand well-spaced houses. ⑥ Nos 2-16. This handsome row has been attributed to the architect George Ledwell Taylor. ⑦ Through **Jason's Trip** (60 Blomfield Road, just off map) you can take the traditional 1906 narrowboat, the *Jason*, on a pretty excursion through Regent's Park and the Zoo to Camden Lock. ⑧ Overlooking the most picturesque stretch of canal, dotted with brightly painted houseboats, **Blomfield Road** and ⑨ **Maida Avenue** are lined with handsome 19thC white stucco houses. ⑩ **Grand Union Canal**, opened at the beginning of the 19thC and designed to link London to the Midlands at a time when the waterways formed the most efficient method of transport. It joins ⑪ the **Regent's Canal**, which runs eight miles through 12 locks to the Thames at Limehouse. ⑫ Among the well-known occupants of villas in **Delamere Terrace** were Victorian writer Sir Edmund Gosse, and Antarctic explorer Edmund Wilson. ⑬ Canal office, a former toll-house. ⑭ **London Waterbus Company** operates a service to the Zoo and Camden Lock from here. ⑮ **Little Venice**. Browning first compared the area to Venice, but the term was not coined until after the Second World War. Surrounded by busy thoroughfares, it is one of the least expected, prettiest parts of the capital, much loved by artists. ⑯ **Tow-paths**, tranquil places to stroll. ⑰ Before **Warwick Crescent** was pulled down and rebuilt in the 1960s, Robert Browning lived at No. 19. ⑱ **No. 2** was a hostel for musicians, where the short story writer Katherine Mansfield stayed in the early 1900s. ⑲ An old Celtic track and later Paddington's High Street, **Harrow Road** was completely redeveloped in the 1960s with the construction of ⑳ **Westway**.

The Bedford Estate

① **Torrington Square**, built by James Sim in 1821-5 on the 'field of forty footsteps', where two brothers fought a duel in the 1680s, killing each other, but leaving behind 40 footprints. ② London University's **School of Oriental and African Studies**. ③ Charles Fitzroy Doll's rambling red-brick and terracotta **Hotel Russell**. ④ **Russell Square** (1800), one of the largest squares on the Bedford Estate; favoured by 19thC lawyers. ⑤ **Malet Street**, now dominated by university buildings. ⑥ **Birkbeck College**, founded by Dr George Birkbeck in 1823 to provide degree courses for people with jobs. ⑦ **Bronze** by Sir Richard Westmacott of the 5th Duke of Bedford, Francis Russell (1809); the Dukes of Bedford owned estates in Bloomsbury and Covent Garden. ⑧ Although Ruskin thought **Gower Street** an architectural disaster, one resident, actress Sarah Siddons described 'the back of it' as 'most effectually in the country and delightfully pleasant'. ⑨ **London School of Hygiene and Tropical Medicine**. ⑩ Charles Holden's monolithic **Senate House** (1932) in Portland stone has a 210ft tower; it contains offices and the University's famous library. ⑪ **Bedford Place**, built by James Burton (1801-5) on the site of Southampton House (c1657). ⑫ **Bedford Square**. Most of the elegant brick houses in Bloomsbury's only intact Georgian square are now the offices of publishers and architects. The central houses on each side are decorated with stucco pediments and pilasters. ⑬ **Nos 34-36**, occupied since 1917 by the Architectural Association. ⑭ **The British Museum** founded in 1753 with a bequest of 50,000 items from physician and naturalist Sir Hans Sloane. The exhibits, ranging from zoological specimens to manuscripts, make the museum the largest and most varied in Britain. Here are the controversial Elgin Marbles, the Lycurgus Cup, Rosetta Stone, Mildenhall and Sutton Hoo Treasures and 2,000-year-old Lindow Man, contained in a huge neo-classical building by Robert Smirke (1838). The British Library's splendid semi-circular Reading Room (1857) has a massive blue iron dome and 25 miles of bookshelves. ⑮ . . . a very handsome, large and well built street, graced with all the best buildings in Bloomsbury' was historian John Strype's description of **Great Russell Street**. ⑯ Bargain cashmere sweaters at **Westaway & Westaway** (No. 62). ⑰ Karl Marx and other scholars penned a line or two as they downed a pint at the **Museum Tavern** (No. 49).

47

▼68

High Holborn/Theobald's Road

① **Lamb's Conduit Street**, named after a benevolent chorister at the Chapel Royal who restored the water conduit in 1577. ② **Great James Street**, a delightful and near perfect 1720s street, lived in at various times by Swinburne, Dorothy L. Sayers, Leonard and Virginia Woolf, and T.S. Eliot. ③ **Cockpit Yard**, where cock-fighting took place in the 18thC. ④ **John Street**, a wide and gracious avenue with many original 18thC houses. ⑤ Disraeli was born at **22 Theobald's Road** in 1804; now Henekey's wine bar (**£**). ⑥ **The Yorkshire Grey** serves real ales brewed on the premises. ⑦ **The Central School of Art and Design** moved into this purpose-built edifice, by W.E. Riley, in 1908. Attached is the Jeannetta Cochrane Theatre, used by the students and named after a teacher at the school. ⑧ **Red Lion Square** was laid out in 1684 by Nicholas Barbon, despite the violent intervention of Gray's Inn lawyers who objected to the destruction of their local 'green belt'. ⑨ **No. 17** was the home of Dante Gabriel Rossetti and later of William Morris and Edward Burne-Jones. A bust of Bertrand Russell stands near the Conway Hall where he used to lecture (now a concert hall). ⑩ **Bedford Row**, unusually wide, was built c1700. It was well restored after bomb damage, though only two original houses (Nos 42 and 43) survive intact. ⑪ **High Holborn** is the main thoroughfare. The dusty office blocks of Holborn, solid and dependable, dominate this area despite its proximity to literary Bloomsbury and the mysterious Inns of Court; this is a place for work not play. ⑫ Perched high on the façade of the **National Westminster** Bank (No. 114) are statues of Edward I (the only one in London) and Edward VII (Richard Garb, 1902). ⑬ The vast late-Edwardian granite mansion of **Pearl Assurance**. ⑭ In front of State House (Nos 63-71) is a bronze, *Meridian*, by Barbara Hepworth. ⑮ **The Russian Shop** (No. 278) sells arts and crafts from all over the Soviet Union. ⑯ **Great Turnstile** (and **New Turnstile**) mark the stiles that kept cattle on Lincoln's Inn Fields (*see page 69*) when they were pastures. ⑰ **The HMSO Bookshop** (No. 49); no government publication is too obscure. ⑱ **The narrow lanes leading to Gray's Inn** (*see page 51*) serve to highlight the spaciousness and tranquillity of the gardens.

HATTON WALL

①

PORTPOOL LANE ②

③

LEATHER LANE

GRAY'S INN

⑥

⑦

⑧

GARDENS

BALDWIN'S ⑩

GRAY'S INN ROAD

⑨

BROOKE STREET

⑪

⑮

HIGH HOLBORN

Chancery Lane
(Gray's Inn)

⑰

⑯ ⑱ ⑲ HOLBORN ⑳

STAPLE INN BUILDINGS

⑳

⑳

⑳

FURNIVAL STREET

FETTER LANE

SOUTHAMPTON BUILDINGS

CHANCERY LANE

◄ 49

50

▼ 70

Gray's Inn Road

① **Gray's Inn Road**, once a link from the north to the City's markets. ② **Portpool Lane**, after Reginald le Grey's Purpoole Manor, which once occupied the site of Gray's Inn. ③ A bustling market in **Leather Lane**, held here since the 19thC, sells everything from fresh fruit and veg to jumpers and pot plants. ④ **Hatton Garden**, on the site of Hatton House, owned by Elizabeth I's Chancellor, Christopher Hatton. Today, the centre of London's diamond trade. ⑤ **Saffron Hill**, part of a 13thC garden, famous for its saffron, used to disguise rancid meat. By the 19thC the area was known as 'Thieves' Kitchen' as young criminals were put through their paces here. ⑥ **Verulam Buildings** (1803-11), named after Francis Bacon, 1st Lord Verulam, who laid out ⑦ **Gray's Inn Gardens** – better known as The Walks – Pepys's favourite spot for a stroll. ⑧ In **Gray's Inn Square**, ⑨ The Hall (1556) was scene of the first production of Shakespeare's *Comedy of Errors* (1594). Bombed in 1941, it was rebuilt by Sir Edward Maufe and still contains a remarkable late 16thC screen. ⑩ **St Alban the Martyr**, built by William Butterfield in the 1860s, and the centre of a Catholic Revival scandal. Rebuilt in 1945 by Adrian Scott. ⑪ The poet Chatterton committed suicide in a house on the **site of 39 Brooke Street**. ⑫ Roman Catholic **St Etheldreda's**, built in the late 13thC as a private chapel. ⑬ **Ely Place**, on the site of the Bishop of Ely's house; a Crown property, it is outside police jurisdiction. ⑭ Delightful 16thC **Ye Old Mitre** pub (Ely Court). ⑮ **Cittie of York**, 17thC wood-panelled pub with cubicles, where clients used to confer with their lawyers. ⑯ Half-timbered tobacconists, **John Brumfit** (No. 337). ⑰ and ⑱ **Holborn Bars**, where silver griffins mark the City boundary. ⑲ **Holborn**, 13thC route for the transport of goods to the City. ⑳ Dickens wrote *The Pickwick Papers* on the site of the vast Gothic red-brick and terracotta **Prudential Assurance building** by Alfred and Paul Waterhouse (No. 142). ㉑ **Statue of Prince Albert** raising his hat to the City of London by Charles Bacon (1874). ㉒ **London Silver Vaults** (53-64 Chancery Lane), warren of subterranean shops in the old Chancery Lane Safe Deposit Co. ㉓ Inn of Chancery, **Staple Inn**, founded in 1378. ㉔ **St Andrew's Church**, 10thC but much damaged and restored. Rebuilt sympathetically in the 1960s.

▲51

▼72

Smithfield

① 18thC **Albion Wireworks**, its exterior decorated with a model lion and unicorn, lit by gas jets for Queen Victoria's Golden Jubilee. ② Art nouveau façade of **Booth's Gin Distillery**, moved here from ③ **Turnmill Street**. ④ **St John's Street**, along which animals were driven on the last leg of their journey to market, once boasted 23 pubs. ⑤ **Charterhouse**, on the site of a 14thC Carthusian monastery founded by Sir Walter de Manny, Knight of Edward III. Built by royal master mason Henry Yevele and, after the Dissolution, bought by Thomas Howard, Duke of Norfolk. In the 17thC, Thomas Sutton converted it into a school for poor scholars and a hospice for gentlemen. The school moved to Surrey in 1872, and the building is now occupied by St Bartholomew's Medical School. ⑥ **Le Café du Marché** (22 Charterhouse Square), excellent French restaurant in a converted warehouse (**££**). ⑦ **Farringdon Station** (1863), original terminus of the Metropolitan Line, the world's first underground railway. ⑧ The **Castle** (34 Cowcross Street), simple pub where the landlord has a pawnbroker's licence granted by George IV. ⑨ **The Fox and Anchor** (115 Charterhouse Street), friendly pub serving breakfast from 6.30 am. ⑩ **Smithfield Ale and Chop House** (334-338 Central Markets). Choose your meat and it will be cooked to perfection on a charcoal grill (**££**). ⑪ **Central Markets**. Smithfield refers to the 'smooth field', where markets, fairs, including Bartholomew Fair, and public executions were held. Sir Horace Jones's Italianate building opened in 1868. Still London's main meat market; not for the squeamish. ⑫ City slickers rub shoulders with meat market workers in the **Bishop's Finger** (9-10 West Smithfield). ⑬ **St Bartholomew the Great**, one of the City's oldest and most memorable churches, was part of a 12thC priory founded by Rahere, Henry I's court jester. It has an impressive nave and 16thC half-timbered gatehouse. Restored by Sir Aston Webb in the late 19thC. ⑭ Designed to link Holborn to Newgate (now Farringdon) Street, **Holborn Viaduct** (1863-9) was the costly but impressive achievement of City Surveyor William Heywood. This ornate bridge, the longest in a series, is decorated with bronze statues representing Victorian virtues. ⑮ **Snow Hill**, notorious for gangs who forced elderly women into barrels and rolled them down the hill. ⑯ **St Bartholomew's Hospital**, better known as Bart's, was also founded by Rahere. Spared during the Dissolution, it was rebuilt in the 18thC by James Gibbs, and is now one of London's most important teaching hospitals.

◄54

▼73

THE CITY

ALDERSGATE STREET

① ② BRIDGEWATER SQUARE

GOLDEN LANE ③

⑤

Barbican ⊖

BEECH STREET

LONG LANE

⑧

ALDERSGATE STREET

⑬

LONDON WALL

LITTLE BRITAIN

▲53

The Barbican

① According to James Howell in the mid-17thC, '**Aldersgate** resembleth an Italian street more than any other in London by reason of the spaciousness and uniformity of buildings'. It was completely redeveloped after the Blitz. ② **Bridgewater Square**, on the site of a house built for Thomas Wriothesley, Garter King of Arms from 1504, but later acquired by the Earls of Bridgewater. The house burned down in the 17thC, and the site was developed by Wren. ③ **Golden Lane**, home of the Fortune Theatre (1660-1) and Thomas Killigrew's school for actors, The Nursery. ④ Although beer has not been brewed at **Whitbread's Brewery** (Chiswell Street) since the mid-1970s, the buildings have been preserved. ⑤ One of London's most controversial examples of post-war architecture, **The Barbican** was designed by Chamberlin, Powell & Bon, and intended to be the residential and cultural core of the City. Concrete towers, linked by high walkways, contain apartments, shops and schools, as well as ⑥ the **Barbican Arts and Conference Centre**. Covering 20 confusing acres (follow the yellow lines), the centre houses the London Symphony Orchestra's concert hall, the Royal Shakespeare Company's two theatres, an art gallery and three cinemas. ⑦ **Guildhall School of Music and Drama**. Founded as a music school in 1880, drama was introduced in 1935, and it moved here in 1977. ⑧ **London Salvage Corps**, established in 1866 to protect insured property from fire damage. ⑨ **City of London School for Girls**. ⑩ A church has stood on the site of blackened **St Giles Cripplegate** since the 11thC. It was devastated in World War II, and restored in the 1950s by Godfrey Allan. John Milton is buried in the churchyard. ⑪ Site of **Cripplegate**, one of the Roman city gates. The name probably derives from the Anglo-Saxon *crepel*, meaning covered way. Edmund the Martyr's body was carried through the gate in the 11thC and held responsible for the miraculous cure of cripples. ⑫ Sir Basil Spence's **Salters' Hall** (1976). ⑬ The well-organized **Museum of London** charts the social history of the city from prehistory to the present. Exhibits range from Roman finds to the Lord Mayor's Ceremonial Coach. (Closed Mon.) ⑭ A section of the medieval city wall stands in **St Alphage Garden**, churchyard of the now vanished St Alphage London Wall. ⑮ In the garden of Brewers' Hall is a charming **bronze sculpture** entitled *The Gardener* by Karin Jonzen (1971).

▼75

55

SEYMOUR PLACE

EDGWARE ROAD

GREAT CUMBERLAND PLACE

CONNAUGHT SQUARE

SEYMOUR STREET

BRYANSTON STREET

EDGWARE ROAD

STANHOPE PLACE

MARBLE ARCH

Hyde Park Place

BAYSWATER ROAD

CUMBERLAND GATE

NORTH CARRIAGE DRIVE

Marble Arch

① The **West London Synagogue**, built in 1870. ② **Connaught Square** (1820s) is a delightful backwater which marks the start of the attractive squares and streets of Hyde Park Estate (off map) once known as Tyburnia. ③ Characterless **Edgware Road** lies along Watling Street, the Roman highway to St Albans, and is still a main route in and out of town. ④ **Al-Madina** (No. 7). Busy self-service café/restaurant offering good samosas, felafel, kebabs and the like (**£**). ⑤ **Maroush** (No. 21) also reflects the strong Middle-Eastern influence in this area and serves tasty Lebanese food (**££**). ⑥ The Edwardian **Church of the Annunciation**. ⑦ Like its continuation, Oxford Street, **Bayswater Road** was an important Roman road. After the rigours of the former, the latter, running the length of the park, seems almost peaceful. It is lined, in the main, with dignified 19thC buildings, and on Sundays lurid paintings are offered for sale along its parkside railings. ⑧ Like Constitution Arch at Hyde Park Corner, **Marble Arch** is marooned on a traffic island, hardly noticed by harrassed car drivers, hardly accessible to pedestrians. Like Admiralty Arch, only royalty (and the King's Troop, Royal Horse Artillery) may pass through its central gates. Designed by John Nash, it stood in front of Buckingham Palace from 1827, but moved here in 1851, and was marooned in 1908. Nearby a plaque marks the site of the infamous Tyburn gallows where, until their removal to Newgate (*see page 73*) in 1783, mass public hangings, attracting vast and clamorous crowds who had been given a celebratory day off work, were carried out. ⑨ At the **Tyburn Convent** (8 Hyde Park Place) an order of Roman Catholic nuns perpetuate the memory, in their constant prayers, of the 105 Catholic martyrs who died at Tyburn. ⑩ The **Cumberland**, vast, conventional hotel near the Odeon cinema. ⑪ If you have an orange box and something to say (that is not obscene, or blasphemous or an incitement to breach the peace) then you can do so by law at **Speaker's Corner** on a Sunday. Alternatively join the hecklers, or just watch the fun.

PORTMAN SQUARE

PORTMAN SQUARE

WIGMORE STREET

EDWARDS MEWS

ORCHARD STREET

GRANVILLE PLACE

PORTMAN STREET

Selfridges

OXFORD STREET

PARK STREET

NORTH AUDLEY STREET

GREEN STREET

LEES PLACE

▲57

▼80

Selfridges

① **Home House** (20 Portman Square), one of only two surviving Robert Adam mansions in central London (1773-7), has a lovely, delicately wrought interior. ② Just to the north in Manchester Square (off map) is the **Wallace Collection**. London's most seductive art museum, it contains the works of art collected by the Hertford family in the 18th and 19thCs. Amongst many European masterpieces it includes perhaps the finest collection of French art, furniture and *objets d'art* outside France, all in the family's palatial town house, left to the nation in 1897. ③ **Jane Packer** (56 James Street). Floral nostalgia from Fergie's wedding-day florist. ④ The **Pontefract Castle**, an exuberantly decorated free house. ⑤ Unexpectedly narrow and prettified, **St Christopher's Place** and **Gees Court** are lined with a mix of pricey boutiques and rather twee restaurants. ⑥ Capt. Benson and Mr Dickson combined to open **Bendicks**, the chocolate makers, after the First World War (No. 55). ⑦ **John Bell & Croyden** (No. 54), 'a hypochondriac's heaven', sells everything from aspirins to blood pressure kits and surgeons' knives. ⑧ The huge but unobtrusive **Mount Royal Hotel**. ⑨ The **Selfridge Hotel**, prestigious member of the Thistle chain. ⑩ **Selfridges**. Built by American magnate Gordon Selfridge (1907-28) this is London's most magnificent store, though it has always lacked the glamour of Harrods. Inside, it has everything, including magical window displays at Christmas. ⑪ Like nearby Green Street and pretty Lees Place, **North Audley Street** is part of the Grosvenor Estate (*see page 81*). It recalls Sir Hugh Audley, the man from whom the Grosvenor acres originally descended via a propitious marriage. Only Nos 11 and 12, designed by Edward Shepherd, remain from the 18thC. ⑫ **Fayrouz**, a typically Mayfair restaurant with over-the-top décor and good Lebanese food (**££**). ⑬ **St Mark** (closed) has an impressively tall Greek portico. ⑭ The **London Marriott Hotel**. ⑮ Long-established shops in **Duke Street** are: H.R. Higgins (No. 79), purveyors of coffee and tea in wood-panelled premises; A. Nelson & Co (No. 73), homoeopathic pharmacy; and Allans (Nos 56-58), a fabric shop where you can buy silks costing up to £700 a yard. At No. 54 is **Justin de Blank's** crowded self-service restaurant (**££**). ⑯ Alfred Waterhouse's **Ukrainian Catholic Cathedral** (1889-91).

Oxford Street/Hanover Square

① On a pretty island site is **St Peter's Church** (1721-4, James Gibbs); much of the original decoration has been removed or painted over. ② **Cavendish Square** (1717), first of the great northward developments by the Cavendish family. ③ Prime Minister Asquith lived at **No. 20** from 1895 to 1908. ④ A glimpse of **Stratford Place**, with the imposing façade of the Oriental Club at its end, revives the spirit after the brashness of Oxford Street. The revamped **Debenhams** ⑤ and model department store, **John Lewis**, ⑥ dominate this street which is otherwise devoted to chain-store shopping. ⑦ Notice the wrought-iron arch erected by Angelo Sedley in 1873 to promote his furniture business, an early example of advertising. ⑧ **South Molton Street**, now a chic pedestrian precinct, was once called Poverty Lane. William Blake lived in penury at No. 17; at No. 46 is Widow Applebaum's, Jewish wine bar and deli (**£**); at Nos 23-27 is Browns, high-profile boutique. ⑨ **Gray's Market** (1-7 Davies Mews and 58 Davies Street). Huge and bewildering stock of antiques in two covered markets. ⑩ **Chicago Pizza Pie Factory** (No. 17), Bob Payton's original all-American pizzeria (**£**). ⑪ Few of the original houses in **Hanover Square** remain but ⑫ **No. 24**, a tall pretty brick house, squeezed by modern buildings gives an idea of how it once looked. To the north of the square is ⑬, a restored **cabman's shelter** resembling a miniature cricket pavilion, and to the south, opposite, ⑭ a huge **bronze of William Pitt the Younger** by Chantrey (1831), which proved too solid for the radicals who tried to pull it down. ⑮ Literary gentleman's club, the **Savile**, with a prettily ornate interior. ⑯ Traditional luxury, complete discretion and distinguished faces are assured at **Claridge's** hotel. ⑰ **Ikeda** (No. 30), expensive Japanese restaurant; sushi is best (**£££**). ⑱ **No. 25**, Handel's home for over 30 years until his death in 1759. ⑲ Although architecturally unremarkable, **Bond Street** has, since Georgian times, been famous for its luxury shops. If you have to ask the price, you can't afford it. Shops in this stretch (New Bond Street) include ⑳ the department store **Fenwicks** (No. 63). ㉑ **Giorgio Armani** at No. 123, ㉒ **Sotheby's**, the auctioneers, at Nos 34-35, and **Asprey**, the famous jewellers, goldsmiths and silversmiths at No. 165 (*see page 85*). ㉓ Funnelshaped **St George Street** with its fine houses (particularly No. 15) narrows at ㉔ **St George's Church** (1721-4, John James). London's first porticoed church, now unfortunately marred by grime.

Regent Street

① **Oxford Circus**, with four identical quadrants designed by Sir Henry Tanner (1913-28). ② Site of the 18thC **Pantheon**, sumptuously decorated and known as the 'winter Ranelagh', where amusements included masquerades, assemblies and concerts. Marks and Spencer now occupies the site. ③ Nash's grand, sweeping **Regent Street** (1817-23); built as part of an ambitious scheme for the Prince Regent, linking Regent's Park to Carlton House (*see page 109*). The most fashionable shops opened in the colonnaded Quadrant, redesigned in 1916. The famous Christmas lights were first switched on in 1954. ④ **London Palladium** (1910) – designed as a luxurious music-hall by Frank Matcham for Walter Gibbons – has been associated with popular entertainment ever since. ⑤ **Dickins & Jones**, fashion and beauty store. ⑥ Black granite, with gilt floral motives, **Palladium House** was designed by American architect Raymond Hood in 1928. ⑦ **Coach and Horses**, 18thC coaching inn on the old Bath road. ⑧ **Great Marlborough Street** commemorates the Duke of Marlborough's victory at Blenheim. ⑨ **Liberty**, department store, set up to import Oriental goods, and famous for its printed fabrics and mock-Tudor building. ⑩ **Cranks** (No. 8), counter-service restaurant for the health-conscious (**£**). ⑪ Seedy relic of the 'swinging sixties', **Carnaby Street** is undergoing a much-needed facelift. ⑫ **Craftsmen Potters Shop** (7 Marshall Street), where the pottery ranges from rustic mugs to full-blown sculptures. ⑬ Reputedly 'the finest toyshop in the world', **Hamleys** boasts six floors, crammed with games, cars, trains, models, robots, animals, dolls and endless other toys. ⑭ **Harry's** (No. 19) serves breakfast to night owls from 10 pm to 9 am. ⑮ **Andrew Edmunds** runs his own charming, simple Wine Bar & Restaurant (No. 46; **££**) with panache. He also owns the fusty print shop next door. Trendy **Sutherlands** (**£££**) is at No. 45. ⑯ Lively wine bar and brasserie, **Shampers (No. 4; £**). ⑰ **Beak Street**, the major part of which was built in the late 17thC by Thomas Beak, Messenger to Queen Mary. ⑱ **Golden Square**, built between 1670 and the 1700s on Gelding's Close and a corruption of the name. A fashionable address in the early 18thC, it was then occupied by foreign legations and declined in the 19thC. Later in the century woollen merchants moved in, and today many of the buildings are let to filmmakers.

Soho

① **Oxford Street**, London's principal shopping street, has been a road since Roman times. ② Melancholy **Soho Square**, laid out in the 1680s, but greatly altered. Notice the French Protestant Church: the French, particularly exiled Huguenots, were the first wave of foreigners to settle in Soho. They were soon followed by many others, giving this endearing area its distinctive villagey yet cosmopolitan flavour which it has never lost. In the late 19thC began its reputation for food (undimmed) and for sleeze (still very much a part, but now in check). ③ The **House of St Barnabas** (1746), a lone reminder of Soho's aristocratic beginnings, with a magnificent 1750s rococo interior (open Wed & Thur). Now a hostel for homeless women. ④ In **Dean Street**, diners at Leoni's Quo Vadis (Nos 26-29; **£££**) can ask to see the rooms where Karl Marx and family lived in disordered poverty (imagination needed) . Pizza Express (live jazz) is at No. 10 (**£**); Red Fort (good Indian food) at No. 77 (**££**); and the cliquey Soho hang-out, the French House, at No.49. ⑤ In **Frith Street** the child Mozart stayed at No. 20; John Logie Baird first demonstrated television above Bahn Thai (No. 21a; **££**); and essayist William Hazlitt died at No. 6, now Hazlitt's, a charming small hotel. Ronnie Scott's jazz club is at No. 47; Alastair Little feeds the media in his eponymous restaurant at No. 49 (**£££**); Soho's Italian population congregate at the Bar Italia (No. 22), with Jimmy's (very cheap Greek) next door at No. 23 (**£**). ⑥ In **Greek Street**, L'Escargot (opened in 1900; motto 'slow but sure') is enjoying its second wind as a fashionable restaurant (No. 48; **£££**); the Gay Hussar still packs them in for its wild cherry soup after 35 years (No. 2; **£££**); and old-timer Maison Bertaux still serves delectable pastries (No. 28). ⑦ **Charing Cross Road** is lined with bookshops. ⑧ Don't miss Patisserie Valerie (No. 44) in **Old Compton Street**, or Italian delicatessen Camisa (No. 61). A knot of similar continental provision stores, as well as fishmonger Richards can be found in ⑨ **Brewer Street**, plus the up-market part of ⑩ jolly **Berwick Street Market**. ⑪ **Shaftesbury Avenue**, London's theatreland, culminates at Cambridge Circus with ⑫ the newly restored **Palace Theatre**. ⑬ **Gerrard Street**, pedestrian-only heart of wide-awake Chinatown. Amazing supermarkets and amusing restaurants abound. Notable are: New World (especially for *dim sum*; No 1 Gerrard Place; **££**); Dragon Gate (No. 7; **£**); and London Chinatown (No. 27; **££**).

Covent Garden

① **Mélange** (No. 59); 'cuisine libre' and crazy 'vandalized' décor (£££). ② **Mon Plaisir** (No. 21), archetypal French bistro (££). ③ An ingenious water-clock heralds the entrance to higgledy-piggledy wholefood enclave, **Neal's Yard**. ④ At **Seven Dials** the original sundial monument has recently been replaced. It was removed in 1773 in a vain attempt to disperse lurking criminals. ⑤ Fringe theatre, the **Donmar Warehouse** (41 Earlham Street). ⑥ Enzo Plazotta's bronze dancer sits at the entrance to contemplative **Broad Court** and the budget **Fielding Hotel**. ⑦ The novelist Henry Fielding lived in **Bow Street** and formed forerunners to the police, the Bow Street Runners when a magistrate at ⑧ the **Courts** in 1749. ⑨ Controversial plans to extend the **Royal Opera House** (dull exterior, wonderful auditorium; E.M. Barry 1858) will mean a three-year closure in 1993. ⑩ **Edward Stanford** (Nos 13-14) has the world's largest collection of maps and travel books. ⑪ The **Garrick Club** (No. 15). ⑫ A converted stained glass factory is the setting for the expensive **Inigo Jones** (No. 14); accomplished cooking, hushed surroundings; (£££). ⑬ **The Lamb and Flag**, a 300-year-old pub with a rough past – it used to be called the Bucket of Blood. ⑭ **The Calabash** in the Africa Centre (No. 38) for hearty African food (£). ⑮ **St Paul's** (1631). Inigo Jones's 'handsomest barn in England' is known as the actors' church, and has wall plaques commemorating thespians from 1680 to the present day. It is all that remains of his great residential square, the first in London, commissioned by the Earl of Bedford. ⑯ Originally a convent garden, Jones's square, always known as the **Piazza** because of its Italianate design, lost its fashionable status when a fruit and vegetable market flourished in its midst. In the 19thC proper market halls were built, starting with ⑰ **Central Market**. When the famous market with its Cockney dawn chorus left for Nine Elms in 1974, the Piazza took on new life as an up-tempo, up-market shopping enclave. Since then street entertainment and swarms of young people have kept Covent Garden humming. ⑱ **Boulestin** (No. 1a), grand French restaurant (£££). ⑲ Cheap and cheerful stalls in **Jubilee Hall**. ⑳ **London Transport Museum**, covering the history of public transport in London; much livelier than it sounds. ㉑ **Boswell's Coffee House** (No. 8), where Boswell was introduced to Dr Johnson (it was a bookshop at the time). ㉒ **Theatre Museum**. A well-mounted tribute to the British stage.

67

Holborn ⊖ ①

KINGSWAY

② GATE STREET

REMNANT STREET

③ LINCOLN'S INN FIELDS

④

⑥

⑦ PORTSMOUTH STREET

⑧

⑩

⑫

HOUGHTON STREET

KEMBLE STREET

KEAN STREET

⑬ DRURY LANE

⑭

RUSSELL STREET

TAVISTOCK STREET

⑮

⑯

ALDWYCH

⑱

⑲

Lincoln's Inn Fields

① **Kingsway**, the main road in the Victorians' final improvement scheme for London (1905). ② **Ship Tavern**, 16thC pub with a priest's hole; haunt of the legal fraternity. ③ **The Soane Museum**, found in three houses that belonged to eccentric architect Sir John Soane, who assembled a miscellany of objects from the sarcophagus of Seti I to Hogarth's *The Rake's Progress* (closed Sun & Mon). ④ **Lincoln's Inn Fields**, one of London's largest squares, laid out on common land. The mid-17thC brick houses, built by developer William Newton, are now mostly lawyers' chambers. ⑤ One of the four Inns of Court, **Lincoln's Inn** was founded in the 14thC and retains its collegiate atmosphere. ⑥ A handsome building with wreathed Ionic pilasters, **Lindsey House** is probably by Inigo Jones. ⑦ **Dickens's Old Curiosity Shop** selling 'antiques and souvenirs' was already 275 years old when he knew it, and has been unchanged since 1700. ⑧ Charles Barry's **Royal College of Surgeons**, which houses the remarkable collection of 18thC surgeon and scientist, John Hunter. ⑨ **Portugal Street**, where in 1661 Sir William D'Avenant opened the Lincoln's Inn Fields Theatre in a converted tennis-court. ⑩ **Royalty Theatre**, built by Bertie Crewe in 1911 as a rival to Covent Garden. ⑪ G.E. Street's 19thC Gothic pile, the **Royal Courts of Justice** or Law Courts, built to amalgamate all the superior civil courts. ⑫ **London School of Economics and Political Science**. ⑬ **Drury Lane**, a fashionable address in the 16th and 17thC, which degenerated into an area notorious for its drunken brawls. ⑭ Benjamin Wyatt's **Theatre Royal Drury Lane** (1811-12) is the fourth on the site. A theatre was first built in 1663 for the King's Company; buildings by Wren and Henry Holland followed. The ghost of a man found murdered in the 19thC allegedly haunts the circle. ⑮ W.G.R. Sprague's **Aldwych Theatre** (1905), home of the Royal Shakespeare Company 1960-82. ⑯ King Alfred endowed the defeated Danes with the land now occupied by the **Aldwych**. ⑰ Wren's **St Clement Danes**, with its Portland stone tower and open spire, topped by a dome and turret by James Gibbs (1719). ⑱ **Waldorf Hotel**, famous for its tea dances. ⑲ **Bush House** (1923-35), planned as a trade centre and now home of the BBC World Service. ⑳ A. Marshall Mackenzie's *beaux-arts* **Australia House**. ㉑ **Statue of Gladstone**, with four allegorical figures at its base (1905), by Sir William Hamo Thornycroft.

69

▲50

OLD SQUARE

① ③

CHANCERY LANE

NEW SQUARE

⑤

⑥ ⑦

⑧

CAREY STREET

BELL YARD

Royal Courts of Justice

⑩

CHANCERY LANE

⑪

⑬

⑯

⑮

STRAND

⑰

FURNIVAL STREET

NORWICH STREET

② ④

FETTER LANE

FETTER LANE

FLEET STREET

⑭

⑱

CHURCH COURT

⑳ ㉑

◀69

▼92

Fleet Street

▲51

① The heart of legal London, **Chancery Lane** is so called because Henry III granted the land to his Lord Chancellor in the 13thC. ② **White Horse**, old coaching inn, where a well-dressed ghost makes nocturnal forays into the cellar. ③ **Lincoln's Inn Chapel** (1619-23) boasts some fine box pews and stained glass. ④ **Printer's Devil**, pub which takes its name from the colloquial term for a printer's apprentice. ⑤ **Ede and Ravenscroft** (No. 93), legal robe-makers, where aspiring barristers also buy their made-to-measure horsehair wigs. ⑥ The saying 'in **Carey Street**' to describe a bankrupt dates from the time when the bankruptcy courts were here. ⑦ Lewis Vulliamy's **Law Society** (1831), with additions by Charles Holden (1902). ⑧ Mock Tudor **Public Record Office** (1851-66) contains records dating back to the Norman Conquest. The museum (open Mon-Fri), on the site of the Rolls Chapel, displays the *Domesday Book*, Guy Fawkes's confession and Shakespeare's will. ⑨ **Dr Johnson's House** (17 Gough Square), where the great man lived 1749-59 and compiled his Dictionary in the attic. ⑩ **Royal Courts of Justice** (*see page 69*). ⑪ John Shaw's Gothic Revival **St Dunstan-in-the-West** (1829-33), decorated with a clock (incorporating two figures that strike a bell), Lutyens' memorial to Lord Northcliffe and a statue of Elizabeth I from Ludgate. ⑫ **Ye Olde Cheshire Cheese**, rambling pub above the crypt of Whitefriars Monastery. ⑬ **Fleet Street's** association with the printing industry dates back to Caxton. It was once lined with booksellers, printers and binders, and until recently all London's major newspapers had their offices in or around 'The Street'. A technological revolution in the 1980s resulted in the computerization of much of the papers' production and a mass exodus of papers from Fleet Street to Docklands and other areas. ⑭ **El Vino's**, a male stronghold despite the 1982 court ruling that women should be served drinks at the bar. ⑮ **Temple Bar**, 19thC memorial designed by Sir Horace Jones. ⑯ **Ye Olde Cock Tavern**. ⑰ Every kind of tea, from Assam to Yunnan, is stocked by **R. Twining and Co.** (No. 216). ⑱ Chillingly romantic **Temple Church**, 12thC with later additions, is circular with a rib-vaulted porch and marble effigies of the Knights Templar. ⑲ Site of the Carmelite **Whitefriars Priory** founded in the mid-13thC. ⑳ **Inner Temple Hall** and ㉑ **Library** by Sir Hubert Worthington.

▶72

▼93

▲52

TURNAGAIN LANE

HOLBORN VIADUCT

SNOW HILL

GILTSPUR STREET

Holborn Viaduct

BISHOP'S COURT

STONECUTTER STREET

FARRINGDON STREET

OLD BAILEY

ST BRIDE STREET

SEACOAL LANE

FLEET STREET

LUDGATE CIRCUS

LUDGATE HILL

SALISBURY COURT

BRIDE LANE

BLACK FRIARS

DORSET RISE

BRIDEWELL PLACE

NEW BRIDGE STREET

▼94

▲53

▶74

▼95

① **Turnagain Lane** once led to the Fleet River (*see page 95*); since no bridge existed there, you had to turn back. ② **St Sepulchre**, last ecclesiastical victim of the Great Fire, which died out just beyond. ③ **Viaduct Tavern** (1869) has a beautiful Victorian interior. The cellars are former Newgate prison cells; that grisly establishment was in its time ravaged by gaol fever, ransacked by the Gordon Rioters, and witness to highly popular public hangings. ④ **Old Bailey** (Central Criminal Court), stage for famous trials since 1539. The present building dates from 1900 (public admitted). ⑤ The elegant three-stage tower is all that remains of Wren's **Christ Church Greyfriars**, destroyed in the Blitz. ⑥ **Site of Fleet Prison**. A barbarous place, it closed in 1842. ⑦ **Le Gamin** (No. 32), most laid-back of the Roux brothers' restaurants (**£££**). ⑧ A row of 17thC canons' houses and a little garden make **Amen Court** a haven. ⑨ **Stationers' Hall**, dating from 1667, with a later façade. ⑩ Samuel Pepys was born in a house in **Salisbury Court**. ⑪ Lutyens's sympathetic headquarters for **Reuters** (No. 85; 1935) stands opposite ⑫ the dominating black glass and chrome **ex-Daily Express building** (1932), with its wonderfully extravagant art deco entrance hall. ⑬ **Old Bell Inn**, built by Wren to succour the builders of St Bride. ⑭ **Punch Tavern**, where *Punch* magazine was conceived in 1841. ⑮ Hemmed in yet aloof, Wren's **St Bride** has a remarkable spire like an extended telescope and has been the model for wedding cakes ever since a Fleet Street pastry cook, Mr Rich, took to copying it in the 18thC. An exhibition in the crypt reveals the intriguing history of the site. ⑯ **Bridewell Place** commemorates Henry VIII's Bridewell Palace, which later became a prison. The demure **prison offices** (1805) remain at ⑰ No. 14. ⑱ **Apothecaries' Hall**, its fine interior virtually unchanged since 1688. ⑲ **Carter Lane**, once a main thoroughfare, has retained its historic scale in an engulfing sea of oversize commercial building. ⑳ Wren's **St Martin Ludgate** is a simple foil to his masterpiece, St Paul's; regrettably, the view of the cathedral from here is impaired by the 1960s mistake, ㉑ **Juxon House**. ㉒ The **west entrance of St Paul's** (*see page 75*) with a dour and dumpy statue of Queen Anne in front. ㉓ The **Deanery** and ㉔ **Chapter House** are also by Wren, the latter marooned by the inept post-war rebuilding around ㉕ Paternoster Square, now undergoing redevelopment.

St Paul's

LOVE LANE

ALDERMANBURY

GUILDHALL YARD

MILK STREET

KING STREET

CHEAPSIDE

BOW CHURCHYARD

BOW LANE

QUEEN STREET

QUEEN VICTORIA STREET

◀ 76

① London's head post office. Upstairs: a riot of colour in the **National Postal Museum**; underground: the unique post office railway linking the capital's sorting offices. ② **Postman's Park**, aptly named oasis with a wall of heart-rending plaques dedicated to selfless late-Victorian heroes and heroines. ③ **St Anne and St Agnes**, a Wren church in appealing domestic style. ④ **St Alban's** church tower, now an office, sole pre-war survivor in Wood Street of the Blitz. ⑤ **Guildhall**, powerhouse of the Corporation of the City of London for 1000 years. The present building dates from the 15thC with an unusual façade and a vast medieval crypt. The bland modern west wing ⑥ houses the **Guildhall Library** (unparalleled collection of documents on London) and the **Clockmakers' Company Museum.** ⑦ Wren's **St Lawrence Jewry**, with bold Corinthian east front. ⑧ **Goldsmiths' Hall** has a massive early 19thC exterior and a suitably rich interior (for details of 'open' days and all other information about the City tel: 01-603 3030). ⑨ **St Vedast-alias-Foster** has a late-Wren (1694) baroque steeple. ⑩ Born of the Great Fire of 1666, Sir Christopher Wren's masterpiece, **St Paul's Cathedral** miraculously survived the capital's second inferno, the Blitz. Ironically, the cathedral's impact has since then been spoiled by ill-considered post-war development. Wren's remarkable output in the three decades which followed the Great Fire totalled 53 City churches, all displaying his rational, yet deeply felt approach to religion; 23 survive today. '. . . if you seek his monument look around you' reads his epitaph under the cathedral's huge dome. There is much to see, not least the famous Whispering Gallery. ⑪ The merchandise in the medieval market of **Cheapside** was organized into individual lanes: hence Bread, Milk, Wood, Goldsmith and Friday (fish) Streets. ⑫ **Le Poulbot** (No. 45), owned by the Roux brothers and still *the* City restaurant (**£££**). ⑬ Anyone living within the sound of Bow Bells, which ring out from Wren's marvellous steeple of **St Mary-le-Bow**, can call themselves a true Cockney. ⑭ **Bow Wine Vaults** (10 Bow Churchyard), wine merchant and wine bar – one of the City's old favourites. ⑮ **City Information Centre.** ⑯ **Bracken House** (Sir Albert Richardson, 1956), the first post-war building to be listed. ⑰ Wren's **St Mary Aldermary**. ⑱ **Sweetings** (No. 39). Fish, shellfish and sandwiches; unchanged since 1830 (**££**).

Bank of England

① **Basinghall Street**, where onlookers used to stare in incredulity at Sir Walter Raleigh smoking a pipe. ② **The Institute of Chartered Accountants**, by John Belcher, 1889. ③ **Austin Friars** recalls the powerful Augustinian monastery which stood here from 1253. ④ The surviving Wren tower of **St Olave Jewry** is now part of an office complex. ⑤ **Old Jewry** was the medieval home of the City's Jewish merchants. Driven out by Edward I, they returned in the 17thC. ⑥ Terraced Adam houses in **Frederick's Place**: a little spot of orderliness amid the jungle. ⑦ Wren's **St Margaret Lothbury**, notable for its fine 17thC woodwork. Next door notice No. 7, Victorian architecture at its most imaginative. Opposite, at the financial heart of the City, is ⑧ the **Bank of England**. The street walls are all that remain of Sir John Soane's first 'Old Lady of Threadneedle Street', a masterpiece, which later gave way to Sir Herbert Baker's lifeless 1920s enlargement. ⑨ Since the 1986 'Big Bang' the **Stock Exchange** floor, once crazy with activity, has lain all but deserted. ⑩ The bankers' **City Club**, a refreshing and suitably clubby piece of Italianate by Philip Hardwick, 1833. ⑪ Turretted High Victorian **Mappin & Webb** (jewellers) has been saved from Mies van der Rohe's 'glass stump' but may yet fall prey to developers' dreams. ⑫ Lutyens's superb 1920s **Midland Bank** has grand marbled halls. ⑬ **Mansion House**, the Lord Mayor's official residence. Its unwieldy façade is by George Dance the Elder, 1739-52. The interior is worth the tour, especially the Egyptian Hall. ⑭ Founded by Sir Thomas Gresham in 1566 for international commerce, the **Royal Exchange** is now home to LIFFE, the Financial Futures Exchange. The present building dates from 1841. Worth a visit for some old-fashioned dealing, frenzied hand signals and all, on the trading floor. Along Cornhill, site of Roman London's forum and basilica, two Wren churches, **St Michael** ⑮ and St Peter ⑯ back onto a medieval maze of tiny alleys which surround the quiet church garden. ⑰ The remains of the Roman **Temple of Mithras**. ⑱ **St Stephen Walbrook**, one of Wren's most rewarding churches with beautiful dome and rich interior. ⑲ Nicholas Hawksmoor's arresting **St Mary Woolnoth**, strikingly different from any of his other strangely spookey churches, but no less lovely. ⑳ **Lombard Street**, named for the Italian bankers who traded here in the Middle Ages. ㉑ **St Edmund the King**, Wren again, but not a show-piece.

Notting Hill Gate

① **Chepstow Villas**, ② **Pembridge Crescent**, ③ **Pembridge Villas** and ④ **Pembridge Square** were all part of the Ladbroke Estate, owned and developed in the mid-19thC by James Weller Ladbroke, and leased to a Hereford man, W.K. Jenkins, who remembered his local towns in their names. Ladbroke planned the area as a 'garden city' and lined the streets with grand villas. His scheme included the Hippodrome racecourse, an unmitigated disaster, built by John Whyte around Ladbroke Grove. ⑤ London's most famous street market is held every Saturday in **Portobello Road**. It dates back to the 19thC, when gypsies traded horses here for the nearby racecourse. With the closure of the Caledonian Market in 1948, the antique dealers flocked in, and today the street is lined with stalls that sell everything from quality silver to bric-à-brac, second-hand records to fruit and veg. ⑥ **Kensington Park Road** was given its smart name in the 1840s, in the hope that it would lure the *beau monde* to an unfashionable address. ⑦ **Sun in Splendour**, friendly local, where in summer customers spill out on to the pavement. ⑧ The menu at **The Galleon** (No. 35) has changed little in the past 40 years. Firm favourites are steak and kidney pudding, and treacle tart with custard (£). ⑨ **John Oliver** (No. 33), interior designer who pioneered foil wallpaper in the 1960s. ⑩ Excellent selection of second-hand clothes for men at **John Burke & Partners** (No. 20). ⑪ **Savvas Kebab House** (No. 7), over 30 years old and still run by Savvas, an expansive Cypriot (£). ⑫ Above the Prince Albert pub, the fringe **Gate Theatre Club** excels in discovering new talent. ⑬ Until the 19thC, **Notting Hill Gate** was farmland. The gate was erected in the 18thC for the Uxbridge Turnpike Trust. A huge and colourful Caribbean Carnival is held every August Bank Holiday in the surrounding streets. ⑭ **Kensington Church Street** (*see page 101*). ⑮ **Gate Cinema** screens arty films. ⑯ Once the Gaumont Theatre, where Ellen Terry and Sarah Bernhardt strutted the boards, the **Coronet Cinema** still boasts W.G.R. Sprague's Italian Renaissance façade and its sumptuous Louis XVI-style interior. ⑰ **Uxbridge Street**, on the site of Kensington Gravel Pits. ⑱ **Geales** (2 Farmer Street) for up-market fish and chips (£). ⑲ The grand town houses of **Campden Hill Road** were built in the 1860s for the wealthy, who came here for the sake of their constitutions.

Grosvenor Square

▲59

▼103

① **Nos 33** (particularly fine), **35 and 36 Upper Brook Street** are good examples of original Grosvenor Estate houses (see below), most of which have been replaced or remodelled. ② **Le Gavroche** (No. 43), despite its hygiene hiccup still doyen of London restaurants, run by the famous Roux brothers (**£££**). ③ **Dudley House** (No. 100), the only mansion (built in 1827) to have survived the ravaging of Park Lane. ④ **Nos 93-99**, set back from the dual carriageway, are also survivors. In the 19thC all Park Lane looked like this terrace, the fashionable houses embellished with Regency bows and cast-iron verandas. Disraeli lived at No. 93 1839-72. ⑤ **Grosvenor Square**, London's largest, lies at the heart of the great Grosvenor Estate, though today it is sadly devoid of original building or character (save the statues of Roosevelt and, recently, Eisenhower). The judicious Grosvenor family, headed by the Duke of Westminster, have profited enormously from this Mayfair estate (built 1720-75), and their equally prestigious Belgravia one (*see page 121*). Grosvenor streets continue to be as exclusive as ever. ⑥ Eero Saarinen's fussy **US Embassy** (1956-9) is notable for its sheer size rather than its irritating looks. ⑦ The **Britannia Hotel**, recently refurbished executive hotel. ⑧ **Grosvenor House Hotel** (built 1928), flagship of the Trust House Forte group, stands on the site of a celebrated Grosvenor family mansion. During World War II its famous Great Room was used as a mess for American officers, including Eisenhower and Patton; now a ballroom. ⑨ Still part of the Grosvenor Estate, **Mount Street** was entirely rebuilt in the late 19thC; its ornate terracotta-coloured houses recall the heyday of the British Empire. At ⑩ No. 14 is **Bonsack**, over-the-top baths for over-the-top people. From its inception Mayfair was studded with high-class shops. In ⑪ **South Audley Street** are: the Counter Spy Shop (No. 62), the place to go for bugging your worst enemy or foiling your would-be kidnapper; James Purdey & Sons (No. 57), all you need for slaughtering the furry and the feathered in style; Hobbs (No. 29), lavish food shop; and Thomas Goode & Co (No. 19), matchless glass and china shop established in 1845. The interior is sumptuous and two huge Minton elephants stand guard. *The* place for a wedding list. Close by ⑫ the colonial-style **Grosvenor Chapel** is curiously modest for the area. Behind it is ⑬ the delightful, oddly-shaped and secretive garden of St George's, **Hanover Square**.

Berkeley Square

▲61

① **Mount Row**, unusual street of brick town houses, each different. ② **One Two Three** (No. 27), more formal sister to Ikeda (*see page 61*; **£££**). ③ **Bourdon House** (1723-5), showroom for Mallett's garden statuary. It looks every inch the private town house it once was. ④ **The Guinea**, classy Mayfair pub, dating from the 15thC. Its well-known restaurant moved with the landlord to ⑤ the **Guinea Grill** (No. 26) when the lease reverted to the brewers in 1982 (**£££**). ⑥ The influence of its American namesake can still be felt in the dcor and dry martinis of the **Westbury Hotel**. ⑦ **The Connaught,** hotel, restaurant and grill room: much vaunted, unfailingly excellent, but no fireworks (**£££**). ⑧ Poulterers **John Baily & Sons** have been at No. 116 since 1720 when building of the Grosvenor Estate (*see page 81*), on which Mount Street stands, was first begun. ⑨ Royal connections abound in **Bruton Street** with a plaque marking the Queen's birthplace at No. 17, the royal couturier Hartnell at No. 26, the Queen Mother's florist Moyses Stevens at No. 6 and the Duke of Edinburgh's gunmakers Holland and Holland at No. 33. ⑩ **Church of the Immaculate Conception**. Lavish 19thC Jesuit church with a Pugin altar. The favourite choice for smart Catholic weddings. Nearby are tranquil public gardens. ⑪ Stately 200-year-old plane trees and an elegant west side are the saving graces of **Berkeley Square**, otherwise dominated by offices and Jack Barclay's gleaming Rolls Royces. ⑫ *Pièce de résistance* is William Kent's **No. 44**, now the Clermont gambling club, preserved as the finest example of a London town house with a sensational interior. In its basement is Annabel's, the hermetically discreet, ever-fashionable private night club. ⑬ No. 14a, showcase of the imaginative designer **Zandra Rhodes**, especially noted since the 1970s for her evening wear. ⑭ **The Royal Institution**. At the turn of the 18thC chemistry professor Humphry Davy caused women to swoon during his packed lectures on account of his good looks. His successor Michael Faraday conducted his electricity experiments here in the 1830s (laboratory open twice weekly). ⑮ **Red Lion**, delightful old 'country' pub serving real ales and English food. ⑯ **The Greenhouse** (No. 27a), hidden mews restaurant with an international menu (**££**). ⑰ **Zen Central** (No. 10), Chinese *haute cuisine* in minimalist surroundings complete with water sculpture (**£££**). ⑱ **The May Fair**, de luxe hotel with built-in cinema and theatre.

▼105

83

Piccadilly

▲63

① Nowhere can match the quality, cut or price of a **Savile Row** suit. Famous names include Gieves & Hawkes (No. 1), Hardy Amies (No. 14) and trendier Tommy Nutter (No. 19). ② **Cork Street**, where prestigious art galleries abound. ③ **Old Burlington Street** (18thC), main route through the Burlington Estate. ④ **Café Royal**, with its opulent rococo Grill Room (**£££**) in the Quadrant (*see page 63*). ⑤ **Asprey** (Nos 165-169), the ultimate gift shop. ⑥ **Royal Institution**, its classical façade by Lewis Vulliamy. ⑦ **Museum of Mankind**, the British Museum's ethnography department. ⑧ Norman Shaw's **Piccadilly Hotel**, extravagantly refurbished and now known as the Meridien. Its sumptuous Edwardian Oak Room Restaurant boasts a Michelin star (**£££**). ⑨ **Bentley's**, authentic old oyster bar (**££**). ⑩ Civilized wood-panelled **Brown's Hotel**, the best place in London for afternoon tea. ⑪ Among **Old Bond Street**'s chic expensive shops are Ferragamo (No. 24), Chanel (No. 26), Gucci (No. 27) and Charbonnel et Walker (No. 28) for delectable chocolates. ⑫ Charming Regency **Burlington Arcade**, built by Samuel Ware for Lord Cavendish to prevent passers-by from throwing litter into his garden. Lined with exclusive shops selling every luxury, from cashmere sweaters to Irish linen, it is still patrolled by beadles. ⑬ **Royal Academy of Arts**, whose home, Burlington House is a fine example of Palladian architecture. Its excellent temporary exhibitions include the Summer Exhibition, a showcase for established and aspiring artists. ⑭ **Piccadilly**. The origin of the name lies with Robert Baker, a 17thC Strand tailor, who, with money he made from selling stiff collars called 'picadils', built a house, derisively known as 'Piccadilly Hall'. ⑮ **Simpson**, for men's and women's fashion. ⑯ **St James's**. Inside Wren's simple brick church there is a large galleried room with a decorated vaulted ceiling. ⑰ **Hatchard's**, for a huge selection of books. ⑱ **Fortnum & Mason**, luxury grocery store, where assistants in tails sell you anything from *foie gras* to *marrons glacés*. ⑲ Having been measured for his suits in Savile Row, the traditional English gentleman will go to **Jermyn Street** for his shirts and accoutrements. ⑳ At **Paxton & Whitfield**, choose from over 300 different cheeses. ㉑ 1960s **Cavendish Hotel**, on the site of the old hotel, run by Edward VII's friend Rosa Lewis, 'the Duchess of Jermyn Street'. ㉒ **White's**, St James's oldest, smartest gentleman's club. ㉓ **London Library**, founded by Carlyle.

▶86

▼107

GREAT WINDMILL STREET

SHAFTESBURY AVENUE

WARDOUR STREET

⑨

⑧

⑦

LEICESTER STREET

⑥

COVENTRY ST

⑤

④

WHITCOMB

Piccadilly Circus ①

PICCADILLY

③ ⑫

② PICCADILLY CIRCUS

⑬

JERMYN STREET

HAYMARKET

OXENDON STREET

PANTON STREET

STREET

REGENT STREET

⑭

⑮

SUFFOLK ST

⑲

SUFFOLK PLACE

CHARLES II STREET

HAYMARKET

⑯

⑰

⑱

REGENT STREET

ST JAMES'S SQUARE

CHARLES II STREET

PALL MALL

㉓

Piccadilly Circus/Leicester Square

▲ 65

① That perennially favourite meeting-place, **Piccadilly Circus**, lacks all the grandeur that John Nash envisaged for it, though its lawdry image has been smartened up of late. ② London's most famous statue is not in fact of **Eros**, God of Love, but the Angel of Christian Charity, a memorial to philanthropist Lord Shaftesbury. ③ The lovely **Criterion Brasserie** (**£**) and **Theatre**, by Thomas Verity (1870-4). ④ The **London Pavilion** and ⑤ the **Trocadero** were once variety theatres, now restored as shopping and entertainment complexes; the Guinness World of Records exhibition in the Trocadero is worth visiting. Back in Chinatown (*see page 65*) ⑥ **Chuen Cheng Ku** (No. 17) is a vast emporium for *dim sum* (**££**), while ⑦ **Poons** (No. 4) is known for its wind-dried foods (**££**). ⑧ **Manzi's** (No. 1) is an Italian survivor – family run, with an almost pre-war ambience (bustling downstairs, calmer upstairs), and good simple fish dishes (**££**). ⑨ In Chinese **Lisle Street** try perhaps Fung Shing (No. 15; **££**) or the New Diamond (No. 23; **££**). ⑩ Visit the church of **Notre Dame de France** to see frescoes by Jean Cocteau. ⑪ Difficult to believe that characterless, commercialized **Leicester Square** was one of London's first (1670s) and grandest squares. In Victorian times it became *the* centre of entertainment; with the arrival of the movies its famous theatres became cinemas. ⑫ Notice **Paperchase's** rare 18thC shop-front (No. 34). ⑬ The **Design Centre** (No. 28): the best of British design. Behind, at 1 Oxendon Street, is the excellent **Crafts Council Gallery**. ⑭ **Burberry's** (Nos 18-22), the last word in rainwear since 1856. Two fine theatres are ⑮ Nash's **Theatre Royal, Haymarket** (which was once just that) and ⑯ **Her Majesty's**, re-built in 1897 by C.J. Phipps. ⑰ The perfect **Royal Opera Arcade** (Nash and Repton, 1816). ⑱ **New Zealand House**, ugly and obtrusive. ⑲ Had Nash's grand plan (*see page 109*) been carried out to the full, all the surrounding side-streets would have looked like **Suffolk Street** and **Place**. ⑳ Sir Robert Smirke's **Canada House** (1824-7, later messily extended). ㉑ William Wilkins's ineffectual **National Gallery** (1832-8) houses quite simply the cream of European painting; easy to get round with magnificent interiors by E.M. Barry. The new Sainsbury wing is under construction. ㉒ The **National Portrait Gallery**. A fascinating record of what the great names in English history and the arts really looked like. ㉓ The **Crimean War Memorial** (1862) depicts Florence Nightingale and her lamp.

▼ 109

▲66

① ② CECIL COURT

GOODWINS COURT ③

The Covent Garden

HENRIETTA ST

BEDFORD STREET

⑥

⑤

BEDFORDBURY

ST MARTIN'S LANE

④

CHANDOS PLACE

⑭

AGAR ST

CHARING CROSS RD

WILLIAM IV STREET

ST MARTIN'S PLACE

National Gallery

ADELAIDE STREET

STRAND

JOHN ADAM ST

⑧

DUNCANNON STREET

TRAFALGAR SQUARE

⑪

Nelson Monument

STRAND

⇥⊖
Charing Cross

⑨

TRAFALGAR SQUARE

Charing Cross

⑩

NORTHUMBERLAND STREET

CHARING CROSS

NORTHUMBERLAND AVENUE

◄87

▼110

Trafalgar Square/Strand

① The **Salisbury** has a sumptuous Victorian interior. ② **Cecil Court** is a pedestrian haven for second-hand book browsers. ③ **Goodwins Court**, a little slice of the 18thC. The fire-mark (look hard) above the arch shows the buildings were insured and would be saved by the insurers' fire-fighters. ④ The **Coliseum** was built as an Edwardian palace of variety and is now home to the English National Opera. ⑤ If you are with children, head for **Fridays** (6 Bedford Street) for lunch (*££*). ⑥ **Porters** (No. 17) serves traditional pies and puddings (*£*). ⑦ **Rules** (35 Maiden Lane) has fortified English stomachs since 1798 (*£££*). ⑧ **St Martin-in-the-Fields**, apart from its beauty (James Gibbs, 1722), is one of London's liveliest churches (restaurant, concerts, crafts, brass rubbing centre). ⑨ **Trafalgar Square** was first cleared as part of a grand improvement scheme by John Nash, but was designed after his death by Sir Charles Barry (1840). Towering above the pigeons is one-eyed, one-armed Nelson (1843), guarded by Landseer's lions (1867). The fountains were added by Lutyens in 1939. Around the perimeter of the square, much redevelopment is in progress. ⑩ A **statue of Charles I**, dating from his reign, stands on the site of the original Charing Cross. This marked the last resting place of the body of Edward I's wife, Queen Eleanor, on the journey from Nottingham to her burial at Westminster Abbey in 1290. ⑪ A Victorian replica of the **Charing Cross** stands outside the station of the same name. ⑫ The **Strand**, originally a riverside bridle-way, was once lined with Tudor palaces. ⑬ **Shell-Mex House** began life in 1885 as the Cecil Hotel, then the largest in Europe. ⑭ The statues on **Zimbabwe House** by Jacob Epstein caused a furore when they were unveiled in 1908. In 1930 they were mutilated in the name of decency and safety after a male member had fallen off and hit an innocent passer-by. ⑮ The 20thC **Adelphi** stands on the site of an architectural masterpiece by the Adam brothers (1770s), which was a speculative riverside development. Its central terrace of houses was sadly destroyed in 1932. Survivors can be seen at ⑯ **1-3 Robert Street**, ⑰ **8 John Adam Street** (Royal Society of Arts) and ⑱ **7 Adam Street**. ⑲ Attractive **Buckingham Street** was home to Samuel Pepys, first at No. 12 and then No. 14. ⑳ The imposing riverside entrance to York House, **York Water Gate** (now land-locked) is the only reminder of the Strand's palaces.

▲67

▲89

CATHERINE STREET

TAVISTOCK STREET

EXETER STREET

BURLEIGH ST.

WELLINGTON ST.

ALDWYCH

Aldwych ⊖

STRAND

LANCASTER PLACE

SAVOY ST.

SAVOY HILL

CARTING LANE

SAVOY PLACE

VICTORIA EMBANKMENT

VICTORIA EMBANKMENT GARDENS

WATERLOO BRIDGE

Strand/Aldwych

▲69

STRAND

SURREY STREET

⑭

⑮

STRAND LANE

⑬

TEMPLE PLACE

Temple ⊖

VICTORIA EMBANKMENT

RIVER THAMES
KING'S REACH

▼113

① **Luigi's** (No. 15) has average Italian food, lots of pzazz, and walls crammed with photos of its board-treading patrons. ② Also theatrical, indeed positively star-studded, **Orso** (No. 27) sports a stylish Mediterranean interior, and the best modern Italian food in town (**£££**). Around the corner its older brother ③ **Joe Allen's** (No. 13) provides *bonhomie*, American food and more well-known faces to spot. ④ **The Strand Palace Hotel** is huge and excellent value, though there is no room service. ⑤ **The Lyceum** was the scene of actor Henry Irving's greatest triumphs. ⑥ W.G.R. Sprague's twin theatres, the **Strand** and **Aldwych** (*see page 69*) flank ⑦ the **Waldorf Hotel**, whose Palm Court teas and tea dances are still a perfect afternoon treat. ⑧ The crescent-shaped **Aldwych** (*see page 69*) links the Strand (*see page 89*) to Kingsway. ⑨ James Gibbs's delectable little baroque church, **St Mary-le-Strand** (1717). Battered by pelting traffic and a wartime bomb, it hangs grimly on, with the help of extensive restoration. ⑩ **Simpson's-in-the-Strand** (No. 100); unchanging bastion of upper-crust Britishness beloved for its excellent roast beef and soggy veg (**£££**). ⑪ **The Savoy Chapel**, intimate setting for society weddings, was rebuilt in 1820 by Robert Smirke, but dates back to the Tudor Savoy Palace. ⑫ Sir William Chambers' boldly classical but dull **Somerset House** (1776). The fine rooms above the *cour d'honneur* now house the Courtauld Institute's Galleries: six superb private art collections (open daily). ⑬ **King's College**, 1829, part of London University. ⑭ This 'Roman' bath (No. 5: National Trust, view by appt) certainly provided very cold plunges for Victorians, but probably not for Romans. ⑮ **Howard Hotel**, extravagant luxury for city-bound executives. ⑯ **Shell-Mex House**, 1931. ⑰ Ever-glamorous, with marvellous art deco accoutrements, the **Savoy Hotel** was built in 1881, next to ⑱ the **Savoy Theatre**, both financed by Richard d'Oyly Carte, the latter for his Gilbert and Sullivan productions. ⑲ **Cleopatra's Needle**, ancient Egyptian obelisk presented to the British in 1819, and finally erected here in 1878. Beneath it was buried a Victorian 'time box', which contained such frivolous items as photographs of pretty ladies, hairpins, cigars and a railway guide.

▶ 92

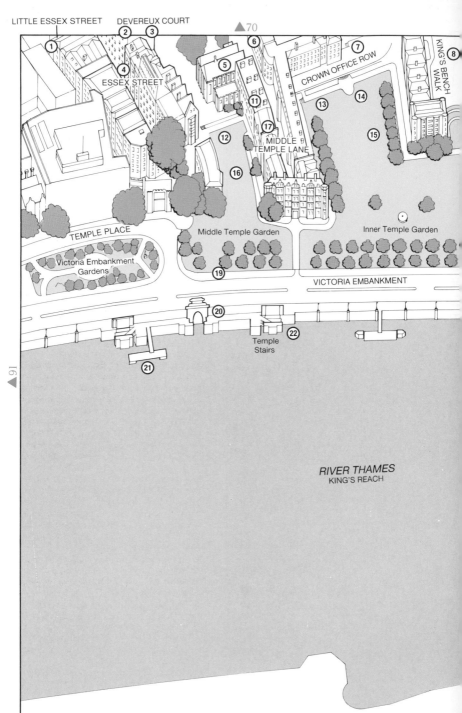

LITTLE ESSEX STREET

DEVEREUX COURT

▲70

①

②

③

④

ESSEX STREET

⑤

⑥

⑦

CROWN OFFICE ROW

⑧

KING'S BENCH WALK

⑪

⑬

⑭

⑫

⑰

MIDDLE TEMPLE LANE

⑮

⑯

TEMPLE PLACE

Middle Temple Garden

Inner Temple Garden

Victoria Embankment Gardens

⑲

VICTORIA EMBANKMENT

⑳

㉒

Temple Stairs

㉑

RIVER THAMES
KING'S REACH

Middle and Inner Temples

▲71

▶94

① **Cheshire Cheese** (5 Little Essex Street), friendly Jacobean pub with beams and an indigenous ghost. ② **Edgar Wallace** (40 Essex Street), a pub on the site of the Essex Head, where Dr Johnson founded the Essex Head Club in 1783. Rebuilt in the 19thC and decorated with Wallace memorabilia. ③ **Devereux Court**, named after Robert Devereux, Earl of Essex, whose mansion, Essex House, stood on the site. ④ **Essex Street**. 17thC speculative builder, Nicholas Barbon, demolished most of Essex Street to build a street of 'taverns, alehouses, cookshops and vaulting schools'. ⑤ **Middle Temple Hall** (1570) boasts a superb double hammerbeam roof and screen, both of oak, and a small table, 'the cupboard', reputedly made from wood of the *Golden Hind*. Readers' coats of arms decorate the walls. ⑥ **Lamb Buildings**, named after Charles Lamb, born in ⑦ **Crown Office Row**, where clerks of the Crown drew up indictments. ⑧ Wren's attractive **King's Bench Walk**. ⑨ The Walls of the aptly named **Witness Box** pub (36 Tudor Street) are papered with cuttings of crime stories. ⑩ **White Swan** (Nos 28-30), local pub for barristers and remaining Fleet Street reporters. ⑪ **Plowden Buildings** (1831) commemorate Edmund Plowden, Treasurer of Middle Temple and builder of the Hall. ⑫ **Middle** and ⑬ **Inner Temples**, named after the Knights Templar, who protected pilgrims in the Holy Land. The Order moved here from Holborn in the 12thC, grew wealthy, was persecuted and suppressed in the early 14thC. From 1608 law students leased its buildings. Barristers have remained here ever since, organized into two of the four Inns of Court. ⑭ **Wrought-iron gates**, decorated with the Gray's Inn griffin and Inner Temple pegasus to symbolize their friendship, stand at the entrace to ⑮ **Inner Temple Garden**, once scene of the Royal Horticultural Society Flower Show. ⑯ **Middle Temple Garden**, where the rival Dukes of Lancaster and York allegedly picked the red and white roses that became emblems of the Wars of the Roses. ⑰ **Middle Temple Library** (1956), by Sir Edward Maufe. ⑱ **Carmelite Street**, so-called because Edward I granted the land to the Carmelites, whose immunity from arrest turned the area into a thieves' hideout. ⑲ and ⑳ **Silver griffins** with red-veined wings mark the City boundary. ㉑ **HQS Wellington**, the Master Mariners' Livery Hall. ㉒ **Temple Stairs**, from where, traditionally, the Swan Uppers leave for Sunbury every July to mark the beaks of cygnets.

WATERGATE

NEW BRIDGE STREET

BLACK FRIARS LANE

BLACKFRIARS C.T.

QUEEN VICTORIA STREET

JOHN CARPENTER STREET

PUDDLE DOCK

Blackfriars

BLACKFRIARS UNDERPASS

VICTORIA EMBANKMENT

BLACKFRIARS BRIDGE

HOPTON STREET

◀93

Blackfriars

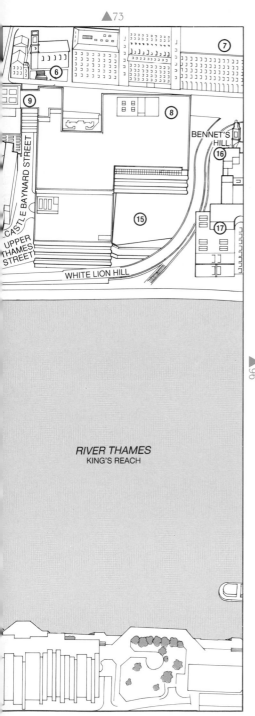

▲73

① **John Carpenter Street** commemorates the Town Clerk of London, whose bequest in 1442 began the City of London School for Boys (see 17). ② **Unilever House**, a conspicuous 1930s building ornamented with statues. Near here stood the house of Dr Budd, where 14-year-old Emma Lyon, later Lady Hamilton, was housemaid. ③ Until Victorian times, the Thames was London's busiest thoroughfare. This street, **Watergate**, marks the old foreshore (before the Embankment was created), and one of the many watergates (this was for Bridewell Palace, *page 73*) where barges could be boarded and alighted. ④ The **Blackfriar**, an amazing wedge-shaped pub in the Arts and Crafts style. Its marble and bronze saloon bar has bronze friezes of monks; the 'side-chapel' bar is even more ornate, with an arched mosaic ceiling. ⑤ **Printing House Square**, site of *The Times* newspaper premises from its inception in 1788, until it moved in 1974. The huge sundial is by Henry Moore. ⑥ The last, plainest and cheapest of Wren's City churches, **St Andrew-by-the-Wardrobe** was built in 1685. Its name derives from the nearby King's Wardrobe where Edward I's ceremonial robes were kept. ⑦ **Faraday Building** (1933) is an early example of the many obtrusive buildings which have crept into the City's skyline in the 20thC. **Baynard House**, ⑧ is another. At one corner, No. 135 is ⑨ the **Telecom Technology Showcase** (open Mon-Fri). ⑩ **Blackfriars Bridge**: built 1760, replaced 1860; widened 1910. The River Fleet, from Hampstead, once flowed into the Thames here; now it is covered by Farringdon Street. The **western railway bridge** ⑪ (impressive cast-iron columns) was built at the same time as the road bridge (both Joseph Cubitt); the eastern one ⑫ some 20 years later. ⑬ **Blackfriars Station**, one of a string built by the Victorians (1864), but now superceded by the adjoining underground station. Blackfriars takes its name from a prosperous Dominican monastery, which stood on this land until the Dissolution in 1538. ⑭ Sir Bernard Miles's **Mermaid Theatre**, launched in 1959 (bar and restaurant). ⑮ The **site of Baynard's Castle**, first built by a companion of William the Conqueror. Subsequently rebuilt three times, it became a royal residence, and was finally destroyed in the Great Fire in 1666. ⑯ **St Benet**, a Wren gem, c1680, with garlanded windows, a charming tower and simple, affecting interior. Since 1879 a Welsh church. ⑰ The new (1986) **City of London School**.

95

Southwark Bridge

▲75

Mansion House ⊖

CANNON STREET

TRINITY LANE

SUGAR LOAF

QUEEN STREET

COLLEGE HILL

Whittington Garden

UPPER THAMES STREET

QUEEN STREET PLACE

86

SOUTHWARK BRIDGE

① **Distaff Lane**, where the distaffs used for spinning were made and sold. ② Wine merchants from Le Riole in Bordeaux gave **Tower Royal** its name. Edward III owned a mansion here, which contained Queen Philippa's Wardrobe. Neglected by the 16thC, it was used to stable royal horses. ③ Responsible for recording Arms and pedigrees, the **College of Arms** is housed in a 17thC mellow brick building with splendid wrought-iron gates from Goodrich Court. ④ After the Fire, 12thC **St Nicholas Cole Abbey** was rebuilt by Wren in classical style. Although devastated in 1941, it retains some original 17thC woodwork. ⑤ **Queen Street** follows the route of the long-vanished Soper Lane, where the soapmakers lived and worked. ⑥ Imposing 1960s **Salvation Army International HQ**. ⑦ **Huggin Hill** takes its name from the Anglo-Saxon word 'hoggene', 'where hogs are kept'. ⑧ **Beaver House** was the London HQ of the Hudson's Bay Company, which traded in furs and skins from the American Indians. Fur auctions are still held here, and the smell of the chemical used to preserve them pervades the surrounding area. ⑨ Dick Whittington owned a house in **College Hill**, named after the College of St Spirit and St Mary, which he founded. ⑩ **Whittington's** (No. 21), wine bar in the legendary man's own vaulted cellars. ⑪ Wren's **St Michael Paternoster Royal**, bombed in 1944 and rebuilt in 1967, where Dick Whittington is buried – a window depicts him with his cat. ⑫ **St James Garlickhithe**, a Wren church with a distinctive steeple of three stone temples. A mummified body is kept in a cupboard in the vestry. ⑬ The late 17thC **Vintners' Hall** has an anonymous painted sculpture, *Vintry Schoolboy*, on the west wall. ⑭ **Stew Lane**, where whores allegedly boarded boats to cross the river to the stews, or brothels, of Bankside. ⑮ **Queenhithe**, where Queen Matilda built the city's first public lavatory in the early 12thC. In the Middle Ages it was London's most important dock, but declined in the 15thC. ⑯ **Samuel Pepys**, pub in a converted warehouse with good views of the river. The restaurant serves hearty English food (£). ⑰ **Southwark Bridge**, rebuilt by Sir Ernest George in 1912-21. ⑱ **Emerson Street**, location of the replica Globe Theatre, due to open in 1992. ⑲ On the site of a bear-baiting arena, Bear Gardens is home to the **Shakespeare Globe Museum**.

THE CITY

▲76

① KING WILLIAM STREET

ABCHURCH LANE

④
⑧ ⑤

CANNON STREET

⑦

⑥

CLOAK LANE

⑫

⑪

DOWGATE HILL

⑬

LITTLE COLLEGE LANE

⑭

COLLEGE ST

⑮

⑯

✆ ⇄ Cannon Street

COUSIN LANE

UPPER THAMES STREET

SWAN LANE

FISHMONGERS' HALL

ST

㉑

KING'S REACH

RIVER THAMES

㉔

LONDON BRIDGE

▲97

Cannon Street

① **King William Street** (1829-35) commemorates William IV. ② **Lombard Street**. 12thC Italian financiers gave London's prime banking street its name. Attractive medieval signs still hang outside the banks. ③ **Gracechurch Street**, named after St Benet's Grass, a Wren church, later demolished. ④ In a pretty cobbled yard, Wren's **Guild Church of St Mary Abchurch** (1686) has a red-brick Dutch-style exterior and splendid interior, with painted dome by William Snow and genuine Grinling Gibbons reredos. ⑤ **Abchurch Lane**, best known in the 17thC for Mother Wells' bakery and the French eating-house, Pontack's, favoured by the literati. ⑥ **Cannon Street**. The name derives from Candlewick, a reference to the candlemakers who lived here in the Middle Ages. ⑦ **The London Stone** is embedded in the wall of No. 111, on the site of St Swithin's, a Wren Church destroyed in the Second World War. ⑧ **Punters** (5 Abchurch Yard), wine bar and small restaurant (**££**) popular with City brokers. ⑨ **St Clement's Eastcheap**, also by Wren. ⑩ **Eastcheap**, famous for its medieval meat market. ⑪ **Dowgate Hill**, home to several City Livery Companies: ⑫ **Tallow Chandlers' Hall** (No. 4), ⑬ **Skinners' Hall** (No. 8), ⑭ **Dyers' Hall** (No. 10) and ⑮ **Innholders' Hall** (29 College Street). ⑯ Hawkshaw's **Cannon Street Station** (1866), rebuilt in the 1960s. ⑰ **Square Rigger** (32 King William Street), nautical pub. ⑱ **Fish Street Hill**, where fishmongers were permitted to trade. ⑲ **The Monument** (1677), built by Wren to commemorate the Great Fire of 1666. Topped by a gilded urn, the 202ft Doric column is the same height as its distance from the site of the baker's shop in ⑳ **Pudding Lane** where the fire started. ㉑ **Fishmongers' Hall**, magnificent Greek Revival building by Henry Roberts and Sir George Gilbert Scott. Its treasures include the dagger used to kill Wat Tyler, a 16thC funeral pall and a fine collection of paintings. ㉒ On the site of an 11thC church, Wren's **St Magnus**. Through its arch was the entrance to ㉓ **Old London Bridge** (1176). On the site of a wooden Roman bridge, it was made of stone, built up with houses and fortified with iron spikes, where heads of traitors were displayed. ㉔ A new **London Bridge** was built upstream in 1831, but was subsequently sold and transported to an Arizona amusement park in 1971. The present bridge, with three concrete arches, dates from 1973.

Kensington Gardens

(1) Queen Anne held tea parties in her **Orangery** (1704-5), attributed to Hawksmoor. (2) **Kensington Palace Gardens** and **Palace Green**, private avenue built on the palace kitchen garden in the 19thC by Sir James Pennethorne. Its sumptuous mansions, now mostly embassies, earned the road the title 'Millionaires' Row'. (3) Delightful Edwardian **sunken garden** with flower beds and pond enclosed by pleached limes. (4) "The house is very noble, tho not great . . . the Gardens about it very delicious", 17thC diarist John Evelyn's description of **Kensington Palace**. A Jacobean house that became a royal palace when William III bought it from the Earl of Nottingham in 1689, and instructed Wren to improve it. He enlisted the help of Hawksmoor, William Kent and Grinling Gibbons. Members of the royal family still have apartments here, and the State Apartments are open to the public. (5) Handsome Carrara marble **statue of Queen Victoria** by her daughter Princess Louise (1893). (6) When George II opened the 275-acre **Kensington Gardens** to 'respectably dressed people' on Saturdays, the (7) **Broad Walk** became one of the most fashionable places in which to promenade. (8) **Round Pond**, where children sail toy boats and fish for sticklebacks. (9) **Bronze of William III** by Heinrich Baucke (1907). (10) **Kensington Church Street**, once a country lane with a toll gate, now known for its pricey boutiques and antique shops. (11) **Maggie Jones's** (6 Old Court Place), honest English food served in country kitchen-style restaurant. (12) **St Mary Abbots**, founded by the Abbot of Abingdon in the 12thC, but later rebuilt, most recently in Early English style by Sir George Gilbert Scott. It has an unusual vaulted cloister. (13) **Jimmie's Wine Bar** (No. 18), haunt of the Kensington set. (14) **Crabtree and Evelyn** (No. 6), bursting with beautifully packaged, delicious-smelling lotions and potions. (15) **Kensington High Street**, one of London's major shopping streets. (16) **Hyper Hyper** (Nos 26-40), for trendy off-beat clothes. (17) Richard Seifert's **Royal Garden Hotel** (1965) boasts a panoramic view from its roof-top restaurant. (18) **Kensington Market** (Nos 49-53) had its heyday in the early 1970s, and still sells Indian cotton clothes and junk jewellery. (19) **Andronicas Coffee Shop** (No. 35), excellent for coffee and Danish pastries.

Park Lane

▲81

① **Hyde Park** combines with Kensington Gardens to form the city's largest open space – an immense 618 acres – which keeps Londoners breething freely. A royal park since Henry VIII appropriated it (Cromwell sold it off; Charles II took it back), Hyde Park has seen countless pageants, parades, spectacles, duels, firework displays, even the odd pop concert. Its feeling of informality is enhanced by the Serpentine (added 1730s; off map) for boating or swimming (even on Christmas Day for the truly hardy). Don't miss the lovely view from John Rennie's 1826 bridge. ② **Achilles**, Britain's first public nude statue (1882) was a grave embarrassment to the 'women of England', who had commissioned it to honour the Duke of Wellington. ③ **Park Lane** was once just that – a muddy parkside lane. After the improvements to Hyde Park Corner (*see page 121*), it became, from the 1820s, London's most fashionable street. Today it is a dual carriageway lined by well-known hotels. ④ Dorchester House, a 'private palace' built by Lewis Vulliamy for a mid-19thC millionaire, made way in 1931 for the **Dorchester Hotel**. A London landmark, it has recently undergone a multi-million pound, year-long refurbishment. ⑤ Disraeli died at **No. 19** in 1881. ⑥ Marvellous view from the Roof Restaurant and bar of the **Hilton**, particularly as, for once, the 28-storey hotel is not in it. ⑦ The **Londonderry Hotel**. ⑧ The **Inn on the Park**, glamorous, superbly run hotel favoured by stars. ⑨ **Nos 4 and 5** (Les Ambassadeurs Club) are surviving aristocrats' houses now trapped between the Inn on the Park and ⑩ the **Inter-Continental Hotel**. ⑪ Once the first in a row of fine mansions, **Apsley House** (Hyde Park Corner, also known as No. 1 London) stands isolated and almost impenetrable, cut off by the traffic thundering past on three sides. Built by Adam (1771-8), it was later aggrandised by the victorious Duke of Wellington and his architect, Benjamin Wyatt. Now the **Wellington Museum**, it is filled with the Duke's fabulous spoils of war, including an astonishing statue by Canova of Napoleon, put thoroughly in his place. Adam's genius is shown off in the lovely Piccadilly Drawing Room, and Wyatt's in the glittering Waterloo Gallery. (Closed Mon.) ⑫ Decimus Burton's **screen**, designed as a park entrance in 1825, is most elegant but now looks sadly out of place. ⑬ **Equestrian statue of Wellington** astride his heroic horse, Copenhagen (buried with full military honours), by Sir Joseph Edgar Boehm (1888). ⑭ **Statue of David**, a memorial to the Machine Gun Corps, by Francis Derwent Wood (1925).

▲104

▼121

▲82

◄103

▼122

Shepherd Market/Green Park

① **Curzon Street** sports a number of exclusive gambling clubs amongst its terraced houses, notably Crockfords which occupies the magnificent Adam ballroom at No. 30. ② **Brinkley's Champagne Bar** (No. 17c) serves Mayfair's favourite tipple (**££**). ③ The **Curzon Cinema** has wonderfully comfy seats, but the excellent foreign films should keep you awake. ④ **Chesterfield Street**, Mayfair's best preserved 18thC street; little has changed since Beau Brummel lived at No. 4. ⑤ **Crewe House** (c1730, façade 1813), a rare surviving example of Mayfair's grand houses set in their own grounds. It was built by architect Edward Shepherd who laid out ⑥ **Shepherd Market**. A maze of narrow lanes brimming with pretty houses, shops, cafés and pubs, it still retains a strong flavour of its notorious past when it was the site of the bawdy May Fairs. Noteworthy restaurants here include: ⑦ **Tiddy Dols** (55 Shepherd Market) with traditional English food and 'Elizabethan' entertainment aimed more at the tourist than the gourmet (**££**); two excellent Lebanese restaurants, ⑧ **Al Sultan (51-52 Hertford Street; ££**) and ⑨ **Al Hamra** (31-32 Shepherd Market; **££**); and ⑩ for top Malaysian food, tropically decorated **Straits** (5 White Horse Street; **££**). ⑪ **George F. Trumper** (No. 9), gentlemen's hairdresser and perfumer since 1875. ⑫ Many well-known people have resided in Half Moon Street, including Boswell, Hazlitt and Shelley, but none more so than the fictional creations of P.G. Woodhouse – Bertie Wooster and his man Jeeves. ⑬ **Miyama** (No. 38), refined Japanese restaurant with high standards of cooking (**£££**). ⑭ **Langan's** (No. 26). London's most exciting dining room is still buzzing, though there are as many star spotters as stars these days (**£££**). ⑮ Playwright and MP Richard Sheridan lived at No. 10 (designed by Robert Adam), as did General Burgoyne. ⑯ Queue up for the best hamburgers in town at the **Hard Rock Café** (No. 150; **££**). ⑰ The great private houses of **Piccadilly** have given way to clubs and hotels. ⑱ **Cavalry and Guards Club** (No. 127), bastion of bowler and brolly. ⑲ Luxurious extra touches, especially appreciated by women guests, distinguish the **Athenaeum Hotel**. The **Park Lane Hotel** next door, ⑳ is still privately owned, unstinting on art deco style and space. ㉑ **Naval and Military Club**, affectionately known as the 'In and Out', after the words on the gateposts. ㉒ **Green Park** – limes, poplars, plane trees and deck-chairs.

St James's Palace

① **The Ritz**. Lunch overlooking Green Park in the fabulous frothy pink dining-room is a real treat (**£££**). ② **Le Caprice** (Arlington House). One of London's most fashionable restaurants, with the bonus of excellent food, reasonably priced (**££**). ③ **St James's Street**, gateway to clubland, a way of life unruffled by the feminist revolution where gentlemen reinforce their prejudices in comfortable surroundings, including: ④ **Boodle's**. Members watch the world go by from the famous bay windows. ⑤ **Brooks's**. Once notorious for gambling. ⑥ **The Carlton**. Tory stronghold. ⑦ **Oxford and Cambridge Club** where women have a foothold. ⑧ **Army and Navy Club**. ⑨ The **Economist Building,** (No. 25), (A and P Smithson, 1964) successfully complements 18thC St James's. ⑩ **Stafford Hotel**. A club for those who don't have one and preferred by many who do (**£££**). ⑪ **Spencer House**. A Palladian mansion by John Vardy. ⑫ **Dukes Hotel** upholds the best traditions of St James's (**£££**). ⑬ Art dealers abound in and around **King Street**, notably **Spink & Co** (Nos 5-7), and one of the world's great auction houses, **Christie's**, at No. 8. ⑭ Shops providing gentlemen with the necessities of life include: **Lobb's**, (shoemakers of 9 St James's Street), **James Lock & Co**, (hatters, No. 6), **Berry Bros. & Rudd** (wine merchants, No. 3), and **House of Hardy** for fishing tackle (61 Pall Mall). ⑮ Nell Gwynn lived at **79 Pall Mall** and Gainsborough died at **No. 82**, which is part of Schomberg House, whose Queen Anne exterior has been preserved. ⑯ **St James's Palace** was built by Henry VIII on a human scale around four courts. The Gatehouse is the most striking Tudor survivor. ⑰ **Chapel Royal** continues its tradition of fine choral music. ⑱ The **Queen's Chapel** (Inigo Jones, 1627), the first English church in the classical style. ⑲ **Lancaster House**, now used for government receptions, was built for the Duke of York in 1827 by Benjamin Wyatt. ⑳ **Clarence House**, rebuilt by John Nash in 1828, is the home of the Queen Mother. ㉑ A charming **memorial to Queen Alexandra** by Sir Alfred Gilbert. ㉒ **Marlborough House**. Now the Commonwealth Secretariat, it was built for Sarah, Duchess of Marlborough by Wren in 1709-11.

▲86

① ST JAMES'S SQUARE

PALL MALL

② ③ ④ ⑤ ⑥ ⑦

WATERLOO PLACE

⑧ ⑨

CARLTON HOUSE TERRACE

Waterloo Gardens

⑩

⑪

CARLTON HOUSE TERRACE

⑫

CARLTON GARDENS

⑭

THE MALL

St James's

⑰

THE MALL

ST JAMES'S PARK

Duck Island

St James's Park Lake

▲107

▼126

Pall Mall/St James's Park

▲87

Admiralty Arch

THE MALL

Horse
Guards Parade

▶110

▼127

① **St James's Square**, centre-piece of London's most gentlemanly district, St James's. It was developed by the Earl of St Albans in the mid-17thC and has been a stamping ground of the upper crust ever since. ② **Pall Mall**, where the French game of *palle maile* was played with mallet and ball. When it became a fashionable boulevard, the name stuck. Known for its gentlemen's clubs whose splendid 19thC façades predominate. Here are ③ the **Junior Carlton Club**; ④ the **Royal Automobile Club** (with squash courts and elegant marble swimming-pool); ⑤ the **Reform Club** (classically clubby interior round an inner courtyard); ⑥ the **Travellers' Club** (lovely façade by Sir Charles Barry); and ⑦ Decimus Burton's stunning **Athenaeum**. ⑧ Its pair, now the **Institute of Directors**, is Nash, remodelled by Burton, but lacks the purity of the Athenaeum. ⑨ **Waterloo Place** (1816), the grand beginning of Nash's great route, via Regent Street, to Regent's Park. It started from Carlton House, the lavish home of the then Prince of Wales, who perversely had it demolished when he became George IV and decided to upgrade to Buckingham Palace. This Nash splendour is capped by ⑩ the **Duke of York's Column** (Benjamin Wyatt, 1831-4), approached by a broad flight of steps from the Mall. The Duke of York in question (statue by Sir Richard Westmacott) was the second son of George III and is best known today for the nursery rhyme about him. ⑪ Pristine **Carlton House Terrace** replaced Carlton House and was Nash's last work, resplendent, of course, in Doric column and gleaming stucco. ⑫ The **Institute of Contemporary Arts** (ICA) is an avant-garde arts (including film) centre. Vegetarian self-service restaurant (£). ⑬ The **Mall Galleries** exhibit traditional paintings. ⑭ When Sir Aston Webb refaced Buckingham Palace he also provided London with a much-needed processional route in **The Mall** (c1910). On Sundays it becomes a traffic-free promenade. ⑮ The central gates of Webb's massive **Admiralty Arch** (1911) open only for royal processions. ⑯ In summer, the creeper-covered **Citadel**, a wartime bomb shelter, resembles nothing so much as a giant hedge. ⑰ **St James's Park** has all one could wish for from a royal park; even pelicans descended from a pair given to Charles II. Made beautiful and fashionable by him, it was further improved by Nash, whose curving lake (lovely views from the bridge) attracts a rich birdlife.

SPRING GDNS

CRAIG'S COURT

GREAT SCOTLAND YARD

SCOTLAND PLACE

WHITEHALL PLACE

WHITEHALL

WHITEHALL COURT

HORSEGUARDS AVENUE

Horse Guards

WHITEHALL GARDENS

DOWNING ST

WHITEHALL

RICHMOND TERRACE

Cenotaph

Whitehall

▲89

HUNGERFORD
BRIDGE

EMBANKMENT
PLACE

NORTHUMBERLAND
AVENUE

VICTORIA EMBANKMENT

Victoria
Embankment
Gardens

RIVER THAMES
KING'S REACH

Whitehall Stairs

VICTORIA EMBANKMENT

▼129

(1) Though **Hungerford Bridge** (rail) flaunts its utilitarian ugliness, there are breathtaking views from its walkway. (2) **Victoria Embankment**, part of Bazalgette's improvements (*see page 147*). (3) **Victoria Embankment Gardens** are dotted with statues and memorials; concerts on summer evenings. (4) **Whitehall**. Now synonymous with faceless bureaucrats, it is named after the Palace of Whitehall, seat of power of the Tudors and Stuarts. This wide route to Parliament is lined with government offices, powerhouses of civil servants and their ministers. (5) The façade of the **telephone exchange** in Craig's Court dates from 1702. (6) The 13thC **Silver Cross** is packed with civil servants from breakfast onwards. (7) **Old Admiralty** (1725), with a stone screen by Robert Adam. (8) **Ministry of Defence**. (9) **Royal Horseguards**, a Thistle hotel, moderately priced by London standards, with wonderful views over the river. (10) **Horse Guards**, by William Kent, is guarded by motionless troopers from the Household Division. (Mounting the guard takes place at 11.00 Mon-Sat, 10.00 Sun.) The building is best viewed from (11) the **Parade**. This ancient tournament ground, now ignominiously used as a car park, is restored to glory every June at the Trooping the Colour, which has honoured the monarch's official birthday since 1805. (12) **Banqueting House**, Inigo Jones's jewel of 1622. The only part of James I's proposed new palace to be built. It survived the fire of 1698 which destroyed the old palace. A startling building in its day, it is now somewhat dwarfed by the monoliths of Whitehall. The magnificent first-floor double cube-shaped room has a ceiling by Rubens glorifying James I. It was outside the Banqueting House that Charles I was executed, and inside that Charles II celebrated his restoration. Open Tue-Sun. (13) **Gwydyr House** (1722). The Welsh Office is one of the least intimidating of the ministries. (14) The **New Ministry of Defence** hides beneath it a cellar from Henry VIII's time; beside it are (15) **Queen Mary's Steps** which once led down to the river. (16) The **Cabinet Office** (1733-6; formerly the Treasury) is linked directly to (17) **10 Downing Street**, Prime Ministers' official residence since 1732. The Chancellor of the Exchequer lives at No. 11, and No. 12 is the Party Whips' office. (18) Every year on the Sunday nearest 11th November, the 'Glorious Dead' of two world wars are remembered in a solemn ceremony at Sir Edwin Lutyens's **Cenotaph**.

▲90   ▲91

RIVER THAMES
KING'S REACH

WATERLOO BRIDGE

WATERLOO ROAD

SOUTH BANK

BELVEDERE ROAD

CONCERT HALL APPROACH

South Bank

▲92

① **Waterloo Bridge**. In 1939 Sir Giles Gilbert Scott's smooth, cantilevered concrete bridge replaced the much praised original ('the noblest bridge in the world', according to the artist Canova, perhaps a touch over-enthusiastically) which was in danger of collapse. Designed by John Rennie and opened in 1817, it honoured the defeat of Napoleon at Waterloo two years earlier. ② **The South Bank Arts Centre** has been growing since 1951, when post-war London decided to buck itself up with the Festival of Britain (remember the Skylon Obelisk and the Dome of Discovery?). The semi-derelict Lambeth riverside was chosen for the exhibition site, and one permanent building was included amongst the temporary ones: the Festival Hall. Typical of post-war architecture, the complex presents something of a brutalist concrete jungle, and it is to undergo a major overhaul by architect Terry Farrell. Internally the buildings serve their purpose well, knitting together performance spaces with cafés, restaurants, bars, bookshops, galleries and terraces to create a vibrant hub for the arts in London. ③ **The Royal Festival Hall**, with later glass façade (1962-5), has a 3000-seat concert-hall and a complicated internal layout; alongside, under Hungerford Arches is the South Bank Craft Centre. ④ **The Queen Elizabeth Hall** and intimate **Purcell Room** (1967) are smaller-scale concert-halls. On an upper level ⑤ the **Hayward Gallery** provides space for major Arts Council exhibitions. Under Waterloo Bridge is ⑥ **The National Film Theatre**. Immediately behind, its red bubbled edges popping out on either side of Waterloo Bridge, is ⑦ the new **Museum of the Moving Image**, opened in September 1988, an exciting 'hands-on' gallop through the art of the moving image, from Chinese shadow theatre to film and TV techniques of the 21stC. ⑧ A National Theatre Company was first mooted 130 years before it finally took root at the **National Theatre** (Sir Denys Lasdun, 1970-6) with its mesh of useful interlocking spaces and three stages, the Olivier (open), Lyttelton (proscenium) and Cottesloe (courtyard). ⑨ The vast **Shell Centre** (1962) runs along Belvedere Road, named after Belvedere House and pleasure gardens which lay, in the 18thC, on the site of the Festival Hall. ⑩ **Drury Tea and Coffee Co** (1 Mepham Street). All sorts of teas, and 22 types of coffee roasted daily in a huge machine.

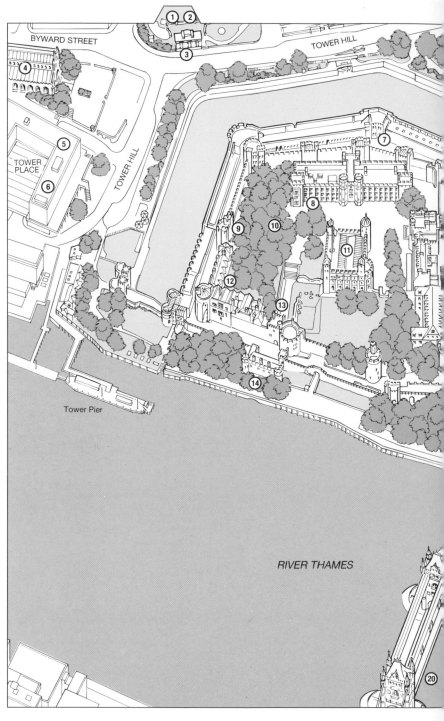

BYWARD STREET

TOWER HILL

TOWER HILL

TOWER PLACE

Tower Pier

RIVER THAMES

Tower of London

① Site of the scaffold on **Tower Hill** where prisoners (see 10) from the Tower were publicly executed. ② Maufe's 1939-45 **Mercantile Marine Memorial** in a sunken garden. ③ Lutyens's tunnel-vaulted pavilion, a 1914-18 war memorial. From here, the green copper roof and steeple of ④ **All Hallows-by-the-Tower** is visible. On the site of a Roman villa, the first church was Saxon. Rebuilt many times, most recently in 1949-58, it contains a magnificent font cover by Grinling Gibbons. ⑤ **Tower Place** (1962-5), concrete and glass pedestrian complex designed by Anthony Beckles Willson. ⑥ **Tiger Tavern**. A new pub on the site of an older one, it displays a mummified cat, supposedly befriended by Princess Elizabeth when she was a prisoner in the Tower. ⑦ **Tower of London**. Britain's most perfect and impregnable medieval fortress, begun by William I, functioned as a palace, a prison, the royal mint, a royal observatory and public records office. It still houses the priceless Crown Jewels in ⑧ **Waterloo Barracks**, guarded by the famous Beefeaters, and is home to six ravens. ⑨ Prisoners of rank were kept in **Beauchamp Tower**, where their carved graffiti survives. ⑩ **Tower Green**, site of the scaffold where prisoners of noble blood were privately executed. ⑪ The oldest building, the **White Tower**, so called after it was whitewashed by Henry III. Many prisoners languished in its dungeons, one of which, Little Ease, is just 4-feet-square. It also contains an armoury and a beautiful Norman chapel. ⑫ **Queen's House**, where Anne Boleyn spent her last days. ⑬ **Bloody Tower**, where the little princes were allegedly murdered. ⑭ **Traitors' Gate**, river entrance used for prisoners brought from Westminster. ⑮ Engineer Thomas Telford's **St Katharine's Dock**, opened in 1828, and the first of the docks to be redeveloped in the 1970s with shops, restaurants and a yacht marina. Telford's arcaded warehouses and Ivory House survive. Among the new buildings are ⑯ the **World Trade Centre** and ⑰ the sprawling but well-run **Tower Thistle Hotel**. ⑱ Site of the **Hospital of St Katharine**, founded by Queen Matilda in the 12thC. ⑲ Wynne's delightful **bronze fountain**, *Girl with a Dolphin*. ⑳ Decorative double-bascule **Tower Bridge** (1886-94), designed by engineer Sir John Wolfe-Barry and architect Sir Horace Jones. Its museum preserves the hydraulic machinery that operated the bridge before electrification in 1976.

Kensington Gore

KENSINGTON RD

ALBERT HALL MANSIONS

EXHIBITION ROAD

Princes Gate

PRINCE CONSORT ROAD

Queen's Tower

South Kensington

SOUTH CARRIAGE ROAD

Princes Gate

8

13

9

PRINCES GARDENS

130

133

① Self-effacing Prince Albert would not have wanted the **Albert Memorial** (1876), which stands in Kensington Gardens (*see page 101*), just west of where the Crystal Palace housed his Great Exhibition of 1851. In Sir George Gilbert Scott's version of a medieval shrine, a round-backed Albert reads an Exhibition catalogue under an enamel-, jewel- and mosaic-encrusted canopy, topped by a spire and surrounded by complex statuary. Undeniably ugly and endearingly over the top, the Memorial perfectly encapsulates the Victorian age. It surveys Albert's vision of a centre of culture and education, only realized, in part at least, after his untimely death in 1861. Ringing the Albert Hall are: ② the **Royal College of Organists**, like a piece of flashy costume jewellery with its mauve and blue sgraffito façade (1875); ③ **Memorial to the Great Exhibition**, with Albert aloft, of course; ④ turretted **Albert Court** (1890), with a novel entrance corridor, and ⑤ Norman Shaw's sweeping **Albert Hall Mansions** (c1880). ⑥ **The Royal Albert Hall** (c1870, by Fowke and Scott, who were engineers, not architects). Albert's crowning glory and London's favourite concert hall, annual venue of the famous Proms, as well as other diverse entertainments from boxing to beauty contests. ⑦ Looking like a displaced country house (it was a private home until 1912) the **Royal Geographical Society** is the work of Norman Shaw in mellow mood (1875). Its engrossing Map Room is open on weekdays. ⑧ 'Like tall thin gentlemen peering at something across the road' was how Leigh Hunt described the stucco terraces of **Princes Gate** (c1850). At No. 25 is the **Sikorski Museum** (open weekday afternoons) in the Polish Institute. South Kensington harbours a large, close-knit Polish community, many of whom patronize ⑨ **Ognisko Polskie** (The Polish Hearth Club; No. 55). Enjoy simple Polish fare in elegant surroundings amongst a charming mixture of bohemians, dignitaries and the occasional cassocked priest (**££**). ⑩ Visit the **Royal College of Music's** exquisite collection of instruments on a Mon or Wed in term time. ⑪ **Imperial College of Science and Technology**, part of London University, is made up of several Albert-inspired colleges. It was redeveloped in the 1960s, save the Queen's Tower (*see page 133*) and Sir Aston Webb's monumental Edwardian **School of Mines** on Prince Consort Road. ⑫ The **National Sound Archive** (No. 29; open weekdays). ⑬ Anyone can stroll across the tree-studded lawn of **Princes Gardens**, owned by Imperial College.

117

HYDE PARK

NEW RIDE

SOUTH CARRIAGE DRIVE

Edinburgh Gate

KNIGHTSBRIDGE

Knightsbridge

KNIGHTSBRIDGE

GREEN

BROMPTON ROAD

SLOANE STREET

TREVOR SQUARE

LANCELOT PLACE

BASIL STREET

PAVILION ROAD

RYSBRACK ST

HANS CRESCENT

HANS ROAD

Harrods

Albert Gate

SEVILLE STREET

WILLIAM STREET

WILLIAM MEWS

LOWNDES SQUARE

LOWNDES SQUARE

HARRIET WALK

HARRIET STREET

LOWNDES STREET

① **Knightsbridge** is the well-heeled shopper's paradise, with plenty of hotels and restaurants to revive flagging spirits. Harrods, besieged by chauffeured limousines, is the centre-piece, beckoning the dowagers, swathed in furs and poodles, from their expensive flats, and county ladies in town for a spending spree. ② **Hyde Park Barracks** (1967-70). Sir Basil Spence's 320ft tower, home of the Household Cavalry, disturbs the skyline. ③ **Mr Chow** (No. 151), 1960s sensation that gave Chinese food a sophisticated image (**£££**). ④ **Knightsbridge Green** is a reminder that this was once a country village. The stocks and maypole stood on the site of ⑤ the **Scotch House** (No. 2), famous emporium of cashmere and tartan. ⑥ Fleeing beneath Bowater House is Epstein's bronze group *Pan*, his last work (1959). ⑦ **Basil Street Hotel** where location, price and old-fashioned courtesy ensure that guests keep returning. ⑧ **The Stockpot** (No. 6). Cheerful, busy restaurant, popular with office workers, (**£**). ⑨ **Sloane Street**, smart shopping street linking Knightsbridge and Chelsea. ⑩ **Harvey Nichols** rivals Harrods for women's fashions. ⑪ **Hyde Park Hotel**, an Edwardian palace favoured in those days by all visiting heads of state, and still bearing up well. Breakfasters have a grand view of the cavalry trotting down Rotten Row. ⑫ **The Sheraton Park Tower**: the higher up the better the room and the view. ⑬ The **French Embassy** was built by Thomas Cubitt for the railway millionaire George Hudson, who later went bust. ⑭ **Richoux** (No. 80) serves delicious sticky teas (**££**). ⑮ **Harrods**. The world's most famous store, by Stevens & Munt (1901-5), grew from a humble grocer's shop. Leaving your dog in the kennels you can arrange a funeral, take books out of the library, have your hair done, marvel at the sculptured wet fish display in the art deco Food Halls, spend, spend, spend, and recover in one of the six restaurants and five bars. ⑯ The **Capital**, a luxurious, intimate hotel with a romantic French restaurant (**£££**). ⑰ **L'Hotel**. The Capital's baby sister is a sophisticated 'bed and breakfast' with a good bistro, **Le Metro**, in the basement (**££**). ⑱ The **Hyatt Carlton Tower** is a favourite hotel of discerning jet-set travellers. Facilities include a tennis court. ⑲ **Lowndes Square** was built by Thomas Cubitt during the 1830s and 1840s as part of Belgravia (*see page 121*),and remains a very smart address.

▲102

▲119

Belgrave Square

▲ 103

APSLEY WAY

GROSVENOR PLACE

DUKE OF WELLINGTON PLACE

HALKIN STREET

▶ 122

BELGRAVE SQUARE

① **Hyde Park Corner** (*see also page 103*), once the western entrance to London, was conceived in the early 19thC as a triumphal approach from Buckingham Palace to Hyde Park. Today it is London's busiest roundabout, its monuments hopelessly marooned by roaring traffic. ② **Constitution Arch** designed by Decimus Burton in 1828, is graced by Captain Adrian Jones's magnificent *Quadriga* (1912) depicting the Goddess of Peace quelling the four Horses of War. ③ The dramatic **Royal Artillery Monument** (C.S. Jaeger, 1920). ④ The former **St George's Hospital** is being transformed into a luxury hotel. ⑤ The **Berkeley Hotel**, complete with roof-top pool, is one of London's most exclusive. ⑥ **Kinnerton Street**, nowadays a great deal more desirable than the slum, complete with open sewer, it once was. ⑦ **Salloos** (No. 62), authentic and excellent Pakistani cooking in a highly civilized setting (**£££**). ⑧ The cosy **Nag's Head**. ⑨ **St Paul's Knightsbridge** has a beautifully decorated interior. ⑩ the **Grenadier**, charming if touristy pub with military knick-knacks and a sentry box outside. ⑪ **Wilton Crescent** (W.H. Seth-Smith, 1827) makes a grand entrance from the north to Belgravia. The north side was refaced in stone early this century. ⑫ **Caledonian Club** (No. 9), for Scottish gentlemen or those with a close Hibernian association. ⑬ **Belgrave Square** is the centre-piece of Belgravia, the later of 2nd Earl of Grosvenor's two prestigious estates, the first being Mayfair (*see page 81*). The brilliantly successful developer Thomas Cubitt, was mainly responsible for the grand white stucco squares and terraces which grew up on marshland here from the 1820s to 1850s. (Cubitt was entirely responsible for Pimlico, later sold off by the Grosvenor Estate.) George Basevi was the architect of Belgrave Square, now mainly embassies. In the centre are nearly ten acres of private gardens. ⑭ In rarefied **Motcomb Street**, the cream-painted Doric columns of the Pantechnicon loom large. Once a huge warehouse and stabling complex, said to be fireproof, it was burnt down in 1874 leaving only the façade. Opposite is ⑮ **Halkin Arcade**, with a façade dating, like the Pantechnicon, from the 1830s. ⑯ The **Turk's Head** and ⑰ the **Star Tavern** (6 Belgrave Mews West) are two more typical Belgravia pubs, with open fires and a cosy atmosphere.

Constitution Hill/Royal Mews

GREEN PARK

▶ 124

▼ 138

① Only very tall or very important people get to see the **gardens of Buckingham Palace**. The former may glimpse the tennis-courts from the top of passing buses, while the latter might be invited to one of the Queen's three annual garden parties. Below the Palace terrace stretches the immaculate lawn, judiciously planted with trees to screen it from prying eyes in the high-rise blocks that are springing up nearby. The lawn sweeps down to a three-acre lake – a noted haven for wildlife, including flamingos. Ornaments in the garden include the Waterloo Vase, standing 15ft high. Carved out of a single piece of Carrera marble, it was supposedly commissioned by Napoleon. The royal 45-acre back garden would be spectacular anywhere, but its position in the heart of London makes it unique.

② **Constitution Hill**. Lined by trees and old lamp-posts, its peaceful quality is marred by roaring through traffic. It was here in 1850 that Sir Robert Peel was thrown from his horse with fatal consequences after visiting the Palace. ③ **The Royal Mews** is architecturally the best bit of Buckingham Palace (*see page 125*) – unadulterated Nash. On Wed and Thur afternoons the public can see the fabulous royal carriages and cars. The stars of the show are the Gold State Coach made for George III in 1762 and always used for coronations, and the Glass State Coach which whisks fairy-tale princesses to their weddings. ④ **The Riding House** was built in 1763-6, with a later frieze and pediment depicting a delightfully spirited *Hercules and the Thracian Horses*. ⑤ **The Grouse and Claret** (14-15 Little Chester Street), classical English food in a quiet pubby restaurant (**££**). ⑥ Henry Gray, author of *Gray's Anatomy*, the definitive medical textbook, lived at **8 Wilton Street** from 1827 until his death from smallpox in 1861. ⑦ Two large unedifying buildings occupy this stretch of Grosvenor Gardens. The first, currently the **Postal Headquarters**, was built in 1956. Its frieze depicts the forces of light triumphing over the forces of darkness. The other is ⑧ **Hobart House**, headquarters of British Coal.

Queen Victoria Memorial Gardens

THE MALL

CONSTITUTION HILL

Queen
Victoria Memorial

Queen Victoria Memorial Gardens

③

①

Buckingham Palace

②

BIRDCAGE WALK

BUCKINGHAM GATE

BUCKINGHAM GATE

STAFFORD PLACE

CATHERINE PLACE

CATHERINE PLACE

BUCKINGHAM PLACE

CATHERINE PLACE

WILFRED ST

⑤

PALACE STREET

STAG PLACE

CASTLE LANE

Buckingham Palace

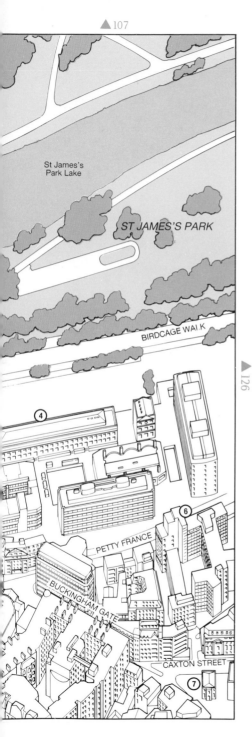

▲ 107

St James's
Park Lake

ST JAMES'S PARK

BIRDCAGE WALK

▶ 126

④

⑥

PETTY FRANCE

BUCKINGHAM GATE

CAXTON STREET

⑦

① In its perfect setting at the bottom of the Mall, **Buckingham Palace** should be a dazzling glory of a building. In fact, the Queen's primary residence is, though stately, very dull. Still, it is the focus of the British monarchy and perhaps the single most stared at building in London. Built as a mansion for the Duke of Buckingham in 1703, it became the family home of George III and Queen Charlotte, and was later aggrandized for his son George IV by architect John Nash. Of all Nash's London schemes, this was his most problematic, and deep troubles over the finances left him disgraced at the end of an otherwise brilliant life. What we see today, however, is not the work of Nash, but of Edwardian architect Sir Aston Webb who, as well as creating Admiralty Arch and the Mall, put a new face on the palace. When the Queen is at home, the flag flies. The changing of the Guard takes place daily at 11.30 in summer, alternate days in winter. ② The **Queen's Gallery** was set up by Her Majesty in 1963 for the public to view changing selections from the incredibly rich and varied royal art collections. Always worth a visit. ③ Designed by Webb, sculpted by Sir Thomas Brock (1911), the **Victoria Memorial** livens up the view from the Mall of Webb's much more mundane palace front. A fittingly sentimental tribute to the Victorian age and its extraordinary queen. ④ The **Guards Museum** at **Wellington Barracks** (closed Sun· *see page 127*) traces the history of the Foot Guards, covering both their fighting and ceremonial roles. ⑤ **St James's Court**, late-Victorian, but expensively refurbished in heavy Edwardian style as the London flagship of the Taj hotel group. Rather incongruously it boasts an authentic and highly-acclaimed Provençal restaurant (orchestrated by top French chef Jean-André Charial), **L'Auberge de Provence (£££)**. ⑥ Little France' got its name when French wool and cloth merchants lived here in the 16thC. The Passport Office is at Nos 70-78 **Petty France**. ⑦ **Blewcoat School** is now the **National Trust Shop and Information Centre**. As depicted by the statue of the blue-coated, shy-looking young boy on the front, it was built – in the early 18thC – as a charity school for local poor children. It closed and fell into disrepair until rescued by the National Trust in 1954.

125

▲108

St James's Park Lake

ST JAMES'S PARK

▲125

BIRDCAGE WALK

② BIRDCAGE WALK

⑥ OLD QUEEN ST

⑨

BIRDCAGE WALK

⑤

⑦ QUEEN ANNE'S GATE

⑧

DARTMOUTH ST

③

④

QUEEN ANNE'S GATE

CARTERET STREET

TOTHILL STREET

PETTY FRANCE

⊖ St James's Park

⑯

BROADWAY

⑱

⑲

⑳

New Scotland Yard

BROADWAY

⑰

VICTORIA STREET

㉑

Birdcage Walk

① In King Charles Street (Clive of India faces St James's Park) is the entrance to the **Cabinet War Rooms**. Though tucked away, Churchill's wartime bunker, laid out as it was then, is well worth a visit (closed Mon). ② **Birdcage Walk** was lined with Charles II's aviaries. Opposite the park are the little gardens and pretty bowed backs of the 18thC houses in Queen Anne's Gate. ③ **The Guards Chapel**, attached to Wellington Barracks (*see page 125*), is a modern replacement for the one destroyed by a bomb with great loss of life in 1944. ④ The **Home Office**. ⑤ Set in a lush garden behind wrought-iron gates, **Queen Anne's Mews** must be the prettiest (private) car park in London. ⑥ **Cockpit Stairs** commemorate the 18thC Royal Cockpit which stood here. They lead up to ⑦ **Queen Anne's Gate**. With Old Queen Street, this is a miraculously preserved 18thC enclave of stone-striped, brown-brick houses (now decorous offices), each with an attractive doorway. Lord Palmerston was born at No. 20. ⑧ A statue of a demure-looking **Queen Anne** marks the place where a wall once divided the street into two closes. ⑨ The **Two Chairmen**, a quaint corner pub established in 1756. ⑩ **Westminster Arms**, popular lunch-time local with a Division Bell. ⑪ **Methodist Central Hall** (1911). ⑫ **Broad Sanctuary**, so named because of the long-gone Sanctuary Tower which once gave refuge to · fugitives. ⑬ **Dean's Yard**, entered through an archway in Sir George Gilbert Scott's Gothic offices (1854), contains ⑭ **Westminster Abbey Choir School** and ⑮ **Church House**. ⑯ **Broadway House** (No. 55) is the headquarters of London Transport (information centre). A 1920s pile, its stone figures of *Night and Day* are by Jacob Epstein, with reliefs by Eric Gill and Henry Moore amongst others. ⑰ **Memorial**, in the form of a bronze scroll, to the struggle of the suffragettes. ⑱ **Stakis St Ermin's**, traditional hotel with much of its late-Victorian character still intact. ⑲ **Villa Claudius**, Italian restaurant where live opera is performed Mon-Fri evenings (No. 10a; **£££**) with an intriguing entrance in front of ⑳ **New Scotland Yard**, the Metropolitan Police headquarters. ㉑ The elongated **Department of Trade and Industry**.

▲ 110

KING CHARLES STREET

PARLIAMENT STREET

CANNON ROW

Westminster ⊖

VICTORIA EMBANKMENT

GREAT GEORGE STREET

BRIDGE STREET

7

LITTLE GEORGE STREET

LITTLE SANCTUARY

127

New Palace Yard

PARLIAMENT SQUARE

8

Little Sanctuary

ST MARGARET STREET

Speaker's Court

6

Commons' Court

5

Star Chamber Court

Broad Sanctuary

Thorney Island

WESTMINSTER ABBEY

9

Westminster Hall

HOUSES OF PARLIAMENT

10

State Officers' Courts

Peers' Court

POETS' CORNER

Old Palace Yard

Chancellor's Court

Royal Court

11

ABINGDON STREET

13

12

Houses of Parliament

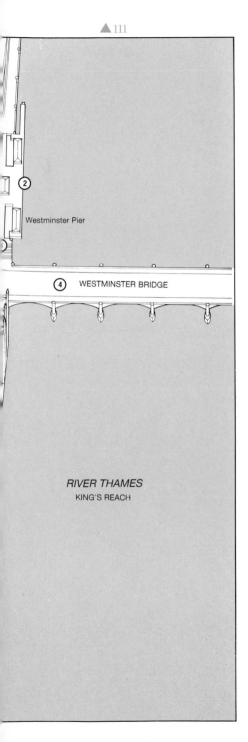

▲ 111

② Westminster Pier

④ WESTMINSTER BRIDGE

RIVER THAMES
KING'S REACH

① The **Norman Shaw building** (1886-90; formerly New Scotland Yard), a baroque castle with a hint of the Highlands. ② **Westminster Pier**, starting point for boat trips on the Thames. ③ Fierce **Queen Boudicca** and her daughters are immortalized in full battle cry in Thomas Thornycroft's bronze. ④ **Westminster Bridge**, perennially favoured viewpoint for photographs. ⑤ Part of the New Palace of Westminster (official title of the Houses of Parliament), **Westminster Hall** dates from 1097, with considerable alterations in the 14thC including the fabulous oak hammer-beam roof. The original Palace of Westminster was home to the monarchy from the 11thC until Henry VIII moved to Whitehall. ⑥ After a fire in 1834, Sir Charles Barry and Augustus Pugin were commissioned to build the **Houses of Parliament** (containing, most notably, the House of Commons and the House of Lords). ⑦ London's best-loved landmark, **Big Ben** has, like the rest of the Palace of Westminster, been restored to its full Gothic splendour. ⑧ The statues of statesmen and heroes in **Parliament Square** are besieged by thundering traffic. Winston Churchill (Ivor Robert-Jones, 1973), remains indomitable. ⑨ **St Margaret's**. The parish church of the House of Commons always attracts star-spotters for weddings and christenings. Much rebuilt since the 12thC, it includes lovely windows by John Piper (1967). ⑩ **Westminster Abbey**. Edward the Confessor established the first great church and monastery on this site – once a swamp – but the present abbey dates from Henry III's time when, in 1245, he conceived the idea of this magnificent stage for coronations and royal burials. Building continued over the centuries, including Henry VII's chapel (1503-12), a miracle of the stonemason's art; and the West Towers by Wren (1745). The memorials to the great and good (and to some who just paid for them) are so numerous that they obscure some of the beauty of the interior, and a sacred atmosphere is hard to maintain given the sheer number of visitors. ⑪ **Little Dean's Yard** contains the main buildings of Westminster School – the dining-room dates from the 1360s. ⑫ The **Abbey Garden** is the fruit of 900 years of cultivation. ⑬ The **Jewel Tower** (1365-6; open to public) is part of the original Palace of Westminster and used to house the king's treasures.

ENNISMORE GARDENS

ENNISMORE GARDENS

ENNISMORE MEWS

RUTLAND GATE

RUTLAND GATE

MONTPELIER WALK

ENNISMORE STREET

COTTAGE PLACE

BROMPTON SQUARE

THURLOE PLACE

BROMPTON ROAD

EGERTON GARDENS

NORTH TERRACE

130

Brompton Road

① In 1913, **Harrods** built its **warehouse** and garage on the site of slums in Trevor Square. Tunnels connect the warehouse with the shop (*see page 119*). ② **Ennismore Arms**, cosy pub in a pretty cobbled mews. ③ Grooming posts still stand in **Ennismore Street**. ④ **Bonhams** (Montpelier Galleries), auctioneers since 1793; good for paintings, furniture, rugs, wine and the odd bargain. ⑤ Until the 1890s, the **Montpelier Street** area was a working-class one, hence the proliferation of pubs. ⑥ T.L. Donaldson's Victorian-Gothic **Holy Trinity Church**. ⑦ Horseshoe-shaped **Brompton Square** (early 19thC) is one of the prettiest in London. ⑧ **Brompton Road** follows the original track from Knightsbridge to the hamlet of Broom Farm (Brompton). ⑨ **Bunch of Grapes**, authentic Victorian pub, complete with snob screens. ⑩ Pretty but pricey, **Beauchamp Place** is packed with chic fashion boutiques, including ⑪ **Janet Reger** (No. 2), for sexy silk underwear, ⑫ **Caroline Charles** (No. 11) for a classic look, **Bruce Oldfield** (No. 27, off map) for stunning evening wear, and ⑬ **Beauchamp Place Shop** (No. 55) for a host of designer labels. ⑭ Starters and puddings only are served at **Ménage à Trois** (No. 15; **£££**); delectable but tiny portions. ⑮ Sit back on a Chesterfield and admire the military prints at the **Grove Tavern** (No. 43). Spot the famous faces at glitzy Italian restaurant San Lorenzo (No. 22, off map; **£££**). ⑯ Set up after the Great Exhibition of 1851 and covering 100 acres, the **V & A** is one of the world's greatest museums of decorative art (*see page 133*). ⑰ Herbert Gribble's extravagant baroque **London Oratory** of St Philip Neri (1878-84), the first important Roman Catholic church to be built after the Reformation. ⑱ With its wood-panelled walls, linen tablecloths and waiters in white aprons, **St Quentin** (No. 243; **££**) feels like a real Parisian brasserie (open every day). ⑲ In a row of tiny cottages, **Luba's Bistro** (6 Yeomans Row; **£**) is one of London's few Russian restaurants. ⑳ **Rembrandt Hotel**, in business since the turn of the century, but now totally modernized.

▲ 116

CROMWELL RD

QUEENSBURY PLACE

CROMWELL PLACE

South Kensington/Cromwell Road

① **Queen's Tower** (*see page 117*) provides splendid views from its top (conducted tours Jul-Oct). ② The department store format of Sir Richard Allison's **Science Museum** (1913) serves its purpose well. Determined to keep up with the times, the museum has recently been revamped and includes popular new exhibitions such as Exploration of Space and the Launch Pad for children. ③ The splendid entrance of the **Natural History Museum**, vast offshoot of the British Museum, lies on an invisible axis with the Royal Albert Hall, marking out the area of museums and colleges nicknamed 'Albertopolis' (*see page 117*). Alfred Waterhouse's Romanesque cathedral to natural science (1873-81) has an impressive stone and terracotta striped frontage alive with animals. Inside, the great iron-roofed nave and long side wings house 500,000 items of zoology, botany, palaeontology, mineralogy and entomology, dominated by the dinosaur Diplodocus in the central hall. Pick your subjects, or interest can flag. ④ The **Geological Museum**, a latecomer in 1935, though founded in 1837, is rather lost between its giant siblings. Worth visiting for its gems and the adventurous Story of the Earth display. ⑤ **The Victoria and Albert Museum**, known to all as the V & A, is the world's largest museum of decorative arts, a wonderfully rich potpourri of treasures. So vast is the museum's hoard – from the Great Bed of Ware to the music room of a St James's town house, from the entire contents of the old India Museum to the Raphael Cartoons – that thousands of priceless objects lie mouldering in storerooms for lack of space. The building itself evolved falteringly from 1856 until 1909 when Sir Aston Webb's glowering façade sealed its identity. Highlights are the beautifully decorated original refreshment rooms, the Italianate terracotta façade of ⑥ **the quadrangle** (Pirelli Garden) and ⑦ the **Henry Cole Wing**. Built in 1863-73, this was incorporated into the museum in 1984 (it contains the lovely Constable Collection) and commemorates its first and greatest director. Go to the V & A prepared to get hopelessly lost, but never bored. ⑧ The **Ismaili Centre** (Sir Hugh Casson, 1983) includes the Zamana Gallery of Islamic culture. Of the museums, only the V&A provides decent food. Alternatively try ⑨ **Paper Tiger** (Nos 10-12) for Szechuan cooking (**££**); or better still, ⑩ **Daquise** (No. 20) a Polish café/restaurant delightfully frozen in time (**££**).

133

EGERTON
CRESCENT

BROMPTON ROAD

EGERTON GARDENS

WALTON ST

BROMPTON ROAD

PELHAM ST

PELHAM PLACE

CRESCENT

PELHAM

FULHAM ROAD

ELYSTAN STREET

LUCAN PLACE

IXWORTH PLACE

POND PLACE

Fulham Road/Sloane Avenue

▲ 131

① **Thurloe Square** (1843): elegant brick and stucco houses by George Basevi surround a tranquil tree-filled garden. ② **Egerton Crescent** is on a grander scale, and was commissioned by Smith's Charity Estate, whose trustees developed the area when the original beneficiaries (Christian prisoners of North African pirates) were thin on the ground. ③ **Walton Street**, charming and narrow, is worth strolling down for its diverse shops, art galleries and restaurants, including ④ the intimate **Ma Cuisine** (No. 113; **£££**). ⑤ Glossy, French **La Brasserie** (No. 272) for light meals and lazy breakfasts with the papers (**££**). ⑥ **Le Suquet** (104 Draycott Avenue), authentic French seafood restaurant; *plateau de fruits de mer* is the crowning glory (**£££**). ⑦ A haunt of young Chelsea is the **Admiral Codrington** (Mossop Street) which, unusually, has a large garden. ⑧ **Michelin House**, magnificent and superbly restored art deco landmark, now the elegant Conran Shop, plus an oyster bar (ground floor) and **Bibendum**, Terence Conran's beautifully designed restaurant, with equally impressive food by Simon Hopkinson (**£££**; first floor). ⑨ Two diverse restaurants in Chelsea Cloisters: **Fifty-one Fifty-one** (**£££**) which introduces Cajun cooking from America's deep south and **Zen**, opulent and very Westernized Chinese (**£££**). ⑩ Sir Nigel Playfair, actor-manager, lived at **26 Pelham Crescent**, one of Basevi's white stucco houses which sweep gently round the immaculate private gardens. ⑪ Now stylish, this stretch of the Fulham Road, opposite Pelham Crescent, is lined with specialist shops such as **English Eccentrics** (distinctive printed fabrics), **The Sleeping Company** (linens), **Divertimenti** (kitchenware), **Agnes B** (timeless French separates for men and women) and **Smallbone of Devizes** designer kitchens, impressively sited in The Old Chelsea Glass Company offices. Through these changes, the original **Laura Ashley** has flourished at No. 157. ⑫ **Meridiana** (169, Fulham Road), a sophisticated Italian restaurant, its roof terrace now glassed in, has been popular since the 1960s (**£££**). ⑬ **Pond Place** marks the route beasts took to the ponds of Chelsea Common, built over in the late 18thC. ⑭ At No. 2a is **Drakes** (**£££**), offering English cooking in a brick-walled, slightly anonymous setting.

▼ 143

135

Sloane Square

① An early red-brick development, innovative after so much white stucco, **Cadogan Square** (1876-90), is the heart of the impressive Cadogan Estate; begun when Elizabeth Cadogan, Baroness Oakley, inherited the Sloane estates from her father, Sir Hans Sloane. ② **Cadogan Place**, tall, gleaming, white houses overlooking spacious private gardens. ③ Across Sloane Street and into Belgravia (*see page 121*), **Eaton Square** is perhaps London's most prestigious address. ④ The **Wilbraham** (No. 1): a genteel hotel with fair prices. ⑤ **Eaton Terrace Mews** typifies Belgravia's many charming mews (formerly stables and coach-houses). ⑥ **The Antelope**, pretty 18thC pub with a hearty clientele. ⑦ **Fenja** (No. 69), a small, elegant town house hotel. ⑧ A cluster of shops to keep Sloane Rangers happy in this section of Sloane Street include the **General Trading Company** (GTC: No. 144), their ultimate store; **Jane Churchill** (No. 135), their favourite mix n' match decorator shop; **Partridges** (Nos 132-134), upmarket delicatessen and supermarket; and **Coles** (No. 131) where they buy their shirts. ⑨ The interior of **Holy Trinity** (J.D. Sedding, 1888-90) is an Arts and Crafts delight. The fine east window, for example, was designed by Burne-Jones and made by William Morris and Company. ⑩ Like its brother department store, John Lewis (*see page 61*) Londoners find **Peter Jones** indispensable. Quite justifiably the John Lewis motto is 'never knowingly undersold'. A model building, too (1936). Notice, on the corner of Symons Street, the idiosyncratic windows of ⑪ **No. 25**, designed tongue-twistingly by A.H. Mackmurdo for Mortimer Mempes in 1893. ⑫ **Sloane Square**, undistinguished in itself, is a focal point and draws together the edges of Chelsea, Knightsbridge, Belgravia and Pimlico. ⑬ **Oriel** (No. 50); crowded brasserie best for snacks such as *croque monsieur* (**££**). ⑭ **Royal Court Theatre**, home of the English Stage Company, who started with a bang in 1956 with *Look Back in Anger*. ⑮ One of the best small bookshops in London, **John Sandoe** (No. 10) is patronized by well-known readers and writers alike. ⑯ Chelsea's bohemian streak still finds expression in the **King's Road**, long after the Swinging Sixties made it famous. Respectable locals mingle with outlandish incomers, especially on Saturdays, and colour and life abound. The road began as a private thoroughfare to Hampton Court for Charles II; all other travellers had to produce a special copper pass.

Victoria

▲ 124

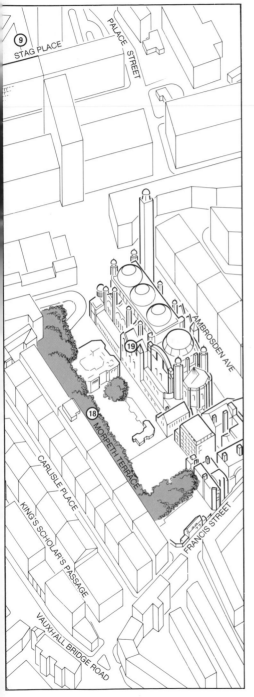

① **The Goring Hotel**, still owned by the descendants of the first, eponymous, proprietor and still noted for its traditional approach. ② Tiny **Victoria Square** is an unexpectedly elegant corner amidst the anonymous bustle of Victoria. ③ Once prey to highwaymen, **Buckingham Palace Road** is today an unexciting thoroughfare. At its northern end are: ④ equestrian book specialist **J.A. Allen** (1 Lower Grosvenor Place); ⑤ **Carriages** (No. 43), a civilized wine bar (**££**); ⑥ **Bumbles** (No. 16) a popular lunch spot (**££**); ⑦ the **Royal Westminster**, one of the reliable Thistle group's more luxurious hotels; and ⑧ **Transalpino** (No. 71), youth travel specialists. ⑨ The mighty aluminium **stag** (E. Bainbridge Copnall, 1962) recalls the once famous Stag Brewery which stood here from the 17thC until redevelopment in 1959. ⑩ The equestrian **statue of Marshall Foch** was presented by the French government along with the two square buildings encrusted with Normandy sea shells. ⑪ **Overtons** (4 Victoria Buildings, Terminus Place), traditional fish restaurant and oyster bar (**££**). ⑫ Built in the 1850s by architect H.R. Abraham, **Victoria Street** was noted for the even scale of its six-storey Italianate buildings. Today hardly an original building stands, and the street is lined with post-war edifices of varying degrees of mediocrity. ⑬ The **Victoria Palace**, built as a music-hall in 1911. ⑭ **The Grosvenor**, modest railway hotel with a typically overbearing Victorian façade. ⑮ **Victoria Station**, built in 1862. Constantly crowded with travellers to and from the south, the Continent and Gatwick, the station gives this part of Westminster its unsettled, transitory feel. In the forecourt is London's largest tourist information centre. ⑯ A thoroughly untheatrical exterior belies the splendidly garish interior of the **Apollo Victoria Theatre**, transformed in 1983 to house the musical *Starlight Express*. ⑰ **Costa Coffee Boutique** (No. 324); 22 types of coffee on sale, plus a small café. ⑱ **Morpeth Terrace** (1890s) was one of London's first purpose-built blocks of flats. Many of Victoria's mansion flats are home to MPs. ⑲ **Westminster Cathedral** is a highly original Byzantine basilica (J.F. Bentley, 1895-1903) with a peculiar striped cladding of brick and Portland stone. The interior decoration has, due to cost, never been finished, but there is an abundance of beautiful marble and, in the side chapels, glittering mosaic. Don't miss Eric Gill's reliefs in the nave, **The Stations of the Cross**. For an easily won birds'-eye view over London, take the lift (in summer) to the top of the campanile.

The Boltons

① In the 19thC, the **Old Brompton Road** wound its way through market gardens and nurseries, and this rural scene is recalled by the numerous 'Gardens' in the area. ② **No. 189** was the home of the soprano Jenny Lind, 'the Swedish Nightingale'. ③ **Read's** (No. 152), a charming flower-filled restaurant serving imaginative English food; the roast beef Sunday lunch is particularly good (**£££**). ④ **Rosary Gardens**, named after a house which stood nearby. ⑤ **Bousfield Primary School**, built on the site of Beatrix Potter's home, won an architectural award in 1956. ⑥ **The Boltons**: these imposing twin crescents, built by George Godwin between 1850 and 1860, contain the most prized of the houses in this exclusive and secluded residential area, a bastion of English family life. With their large gardens front and back, they are still mostly single dwellings; the anglophile Douglas Fairbanks Jnr was once a resident. Although atypical of the London square, The Boltons illustrates the intimate, villagey atmosphere achieved by such an inward-facing design, isolating the inhabitants from the hustle and bustle of the surrounding streets. ⑦ **St Mary-the-Boltons** (also by Godwin), is perfectly set in the central gardens. It has an unusual spire circled with angels and was extensively restored after bomb damage. ⑧ **Tregunter Road**, part of the Gunter Estate, and several of the nearby streets – Gilston, Priory, Gledhow – take their names from places in Wales and Yorkshire where the family had property. ⑨ **The Society of Authors** (No. 84), founded in 1884 by William Besant to promote and defend the interests of authors. Active members in the past have included Shaw, Galsworthy and E.M. Forster. ⑩ **Blakes** (No. 33). Hidden in a Victorian terrace, this exclusive, idiosyncratic hotel is much admired by media folk – stylish and glitzy, it serves good food *à la mode* in the black, mirrored dining-room (**£££**).

▲ 134

St Luke's Gardens

▼ 148

Sydney Street/King's Road

① **The Chelsea Design Co** (65 Sydney St) makes classic English day and evening wear. ② **St Luke's Church** 1820-4, imposing parish church where Dickens was married – an early example of Gothic Revival, by James Savage. ③ The narrow streets of this area, with their glamorized Victorian cottages, have the air of a film-set village, at whose heart, **Chelsea Green**, is ④ **Monkeys** (No. 1), a restaurant popular with well-heeled locals; Anglo-French cuisine (**£££**). ⑤ **Sydney Street** was built in 1845 on Smith's Charity Estate. In 1864 the 'Flying Man', armed with bat wings and a tail, had an undignified crash landing here. ⑥ **Dan's** (No. 119); *nouvelle cuisine* for Sloanes (**££**). ⑦ **The Chelsea Gardener** (No. 125), large expensive garden centre and associated shops. ⑧ **Chelsea School of Art** (sculpture by Henry Moore in the forecourt) nurtures the artistic aspirations of the locals. ⑨ Street-cred clothes shops mingle with fine antique markets along this stretch of the **King's Road**, whilst towards World's End ever more eccentric fashions are brought and paraded. ⑩ **Argyll House**; the first of a row of grand houses, this by Giacomo Leoni, 1723. Recently inhabited by film director Carol Reed. ⑪ **Henry J. Bean's** (No. 195); bar, burgers, floodlit fountain, 1950s American memorabilia (**££**). ⑫ **The Chenil Galleries** (Nos 181-183), specialises in fine arts and rare antiques; note Paul Jones: wonderfully rich antique fabrics. ⑬ **Chelsea Old Town Hall** (1886), listed building by John Brydon with later façade by Leonard Stokes. Inside, murals depict Chelsea's association with the arts, science and literature. It hosts the well-known Antiques Fairs in March and September. ⑭ **Antiquarius** (Nos 135-141), a maze of stalls crammed with every kind of smaller antique – especially good for clothes. Fronting the market are elegant fashion shops, such as Edina Ronay (No. 141), for exclusive women's clothes, and David Fielden (No. 137) for ravishing evening and wedding dresses. ⑮ **The Pheasantry**: the ornate façade, by the furniture makers Joubert, is all that remains of the original building. It was famous as Princess Astafieva's ballet school, while politicians and painters met in the basement club. Now a cocktail bar, with light meals served; tables outside (**£**).

King's Road/Royal Avenue

① **Markham Square** (1836) was built on a field belonging to Box Farm, and named after the farm's last owner. ② **Alexander's** basement restaurant (138a King's Road; **££**), a throw-back to the Swinging Sixties when it was owned by the husband of Mary Quant. She occupied the shop above, from where she spearheaded the fashion revolution of 20 years ago. ③ This section of the **King's Road** is dominated by branches of high street fashion chains ④. At No. 98, is the **Chelsea Kitchen** (**£**), cheap, cheerful, honest and, after two decades, something of an institution. ⑤ **Cheltenham Terrace**, a neat row of 18thC houses facing the **Duke of York's** ⑥, administrative headquarters of the Territorial Army and home to various regimental units. The oldest of its buildings, with a central portico, is by John Sanders, 1801, and was built for soldiers' orphans. ⑦ **Wellington Square**, 1830, the earliest of the many squares which opened off the newly public King's Road thoroughfare, and one of the best – well-detailed houses, fine trees. Named after the Duke, whose brother was rector of Chelsea at the time. ⑧ **Woodfall Street**, a green and flowery cul-de-sac of charming 19thC cottages. On the corner, the Phoenix is a quiet, wood-panelled Edwardian pub. ⑨ Bram Stoker, author of *Dracula*, lived at **18 St Leonard's Terrace** at the turn of the century. This block (Nos 14-31) is considered to be one of the best Georgian terraces in Chelsea (1765). ⑩ **Royal Avenue**, a wide boulevard built in 1692-4 (houses are 19thC), part of William III's unfinished plan to link the Royal Hospital with his new residence, Kensington Palace. Fictional home of James Bond. ⑪ **23 Tedworth Square**, home of Mark Twain briefly 1896-7; now flats. ⑫ **No. 15**, home of two actresses, first Lillie Langtry and later Mrs Patrick Campbell, who received G.B. Shaw's famous correspondence at this address. ⑬ **Burton's Court**, 14 acres of open land, not open to the public; Chelsea Pensioners play bowls and the Brigade of Guards play cricket here. ⑭ 'Quiet, dignified, the work of a gentleman'. Carlyle's description of the **Royal Hospital** founded by Charles II for veteran soldiers (the Chelsea Pensioners with their distinctive uniforms) and built by Wren 1682-92. Chapel, Hall and grounds (*see page 147*) open to the public.

▶ 146

ROYAL HOSPITAL ROAD

CHELSEA BRIDGE ROAD

CHELSEA EMBANKMENT

Ranelagh Gardens

① **Chelsea Barracks**, first built by George Moore in 1861-2 for 1000 footguards, then rebuilt in the 1960s by Tripe and Wakeham. ② **Royal Hospital Road**, originally called Queen's Road and lined with many fine houses, now demolished. ③ The last resting place for Chelsea Pensioners, **Royal Hospital Burial Ground** was consecrated in 1691 and closed for burials in 1854. Among the 10,000 buried here are William Hiseland, a Pensioner who died in 1732 at the ripe old age of 112, and two women who joined the army, and whose sex was only discovered when they were wounded in the Crimean War. ④ **Site of Ranelagh House**, a mansion built c1690 by the Earl of Ranelagh, Paymaster-General to the Forces. After the earl's death, the house and grounds, ⑤ **Ranelagh Gardens**, were bought by a syndicate, and in 1742 the grounds were opened to the public as pleasure gardens. Until they closed in 1803, the gardens were reputedly the most fashionable and elegant in Europe. Gothic novelist, Horace Walpole, claimed: 'You can't set your foot without treading on a Prince, or Duke of Cumberland.' Attractions included music, opera, Venetian masquerades, boating on an artificial lake, stalls selling Dresden, booths serving refreshments, a magnificent rococo rotunda and a Chinese pavilion. ⑥ Grinling Gibbons's bronze **statue of Charles II** dressed as a Roman soldier gave Figure Court its name. On Oak-apple Day, 29 May, the Chelsea Pensioners decorate the statue with oak leaves to celebrate the King's birthday, and his escape from the Roundheads at Worcester, hidden in an oak tree. ⑦ The **grounds of the Royal Hospital** (*see page 145*), designed by Wren as a formal garden have, since 1913, been the scene of the Chelsea Flower Show each May. ⑧ Charles Cockerell's towering **granite obelisk** (1853) commemorates the soldiers who fell at Chillianwalla in January 1849. ⑨ **Chelsea Embankment**. Along with Albert and Victoria embankments, an impressive Victorian achievement (with main sewers below); work of Sir Joseph Bazalgette.

▲142

CARLYLE SQUARE

KING'S ROAD

BRAMERTON STREET

GLEBE PLACE

MARGARETTA TERRACE

FLOOD WALK

PHENE STREET

OAKLEY STREET

UPPER CHEYNE ROW

CHEYNE ROW

JUSTICE WALK

LAWRENCE STREET

OLD CHURCH STREET

CHEYNE WALK

CHELSEA EMBANKMENT

Roper's Garden

RIVER THAMES
CHELSEA REACH

Cheyne Walk/Oakley Street

▲143

▶150

Cadogan Pier

① Osbert Sitwell lived at **No. 2** in leafy, elegant Carlyle Square. ② **Chelsea Antique Market** (Nos 245-253), good for bargains, bric-à-brac and books. ③ **No. 215**, attractive brick house (1720), occupied by Dr T. Arne, composer of *Rule Britannia*, and later by actress Ellen Terry. ④ Charles Kingsley, author of *The Water Babies*, lived at **St Luke's Rectory** (56 Old Church Street) as a child. ⑤ **Phené Arms**, one of Chelsea's oldest pubs, built by local eccentric, Dr Phené ⑥ Pretty, flat-fronted **22 Upper Cheyne Row** was home of critic Leigh Hunt. ⑦ Roman Catholic **Church of St Thomas More** (1895), built on the site of a William de Morgan pottery. ⑧ In the mid-18thC, picaresque novelist Smollett lived at **16 Lawrence Street**, which also housed the Chelsea China factory. ⑨ **Grey House Books** (No. 12a), charming antiquarian bookshop. ⑩ . . . flag-pathed, sunk-storied, iron-railed, all old-fashioned': Scottish historian and philosopher Thomas Carlyle's description of Cheyne Row, where he lived at ⑪ **No. 24**, a handsome Queen Anne house crammed with his possessions (open in summer). ⑫ **Oakley Street**, built on the Cadogan Estate in the 1850s. Oscar Wilde sought refuge with his mother and brother at No. 87 during his persecution; Antarctic explorer, Robert Falcon Scott, lived at No. 56. ⑬ **Old Church Street**, Chelsea's oldest thoroughfare. ⑭ **H. Allen Smith** (No. 26), wine merchants since 1832, originally occupied the old court-house in Justice Walk ⑮, where the cells were used as cellars. ⑯ **Crosby Hall** (fine hammerbeam roof, plus Holbein's *Sir Thomas More and Family*) is the great hall of a 15thC mansion, moved here piecemeal from Bishopsgate in 1910 to escape demolition (open daily). ⑰ **Roper's Gardens**, named after More's daughter, Margaret Roper. ⑱ Before their state wedding, Henry VIII married Jane Seymour in **Chelsea Old Church** (1157, but much rebuilt). ⑲ 400-year-old pub, **King's Head and Eight Bells**. ⑳ The recently opened Cadogan Brasserie (Nos 31-37; **££**). Outside is ㉑ Wynne's graceful sculpture *Boy with a Dolphin*. ㉒ **Nos 19-26**, site of Henry VIII's manor house. Mulberry trees said to be planted by Elizabeth I can be glimpsed through the arch of No. 24. ㉓ **No. 16**, home of Rossetti and Swinburne, who lived with a menagerie of exotic animals, including peacocks whose screeches disturbed the neighbours. ㉔ **Albert Bridge**, Ordish's pretty cantilever and suspension bridge, with tollhouses still intact (1873).

▲ 144

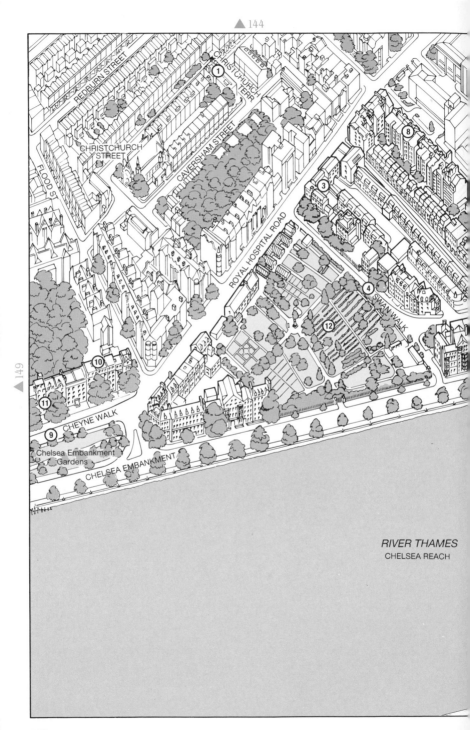

▲ 149

RIVER THAMES
CHELSEA REACH

Royal Hospital Road/Chelsea Embankment

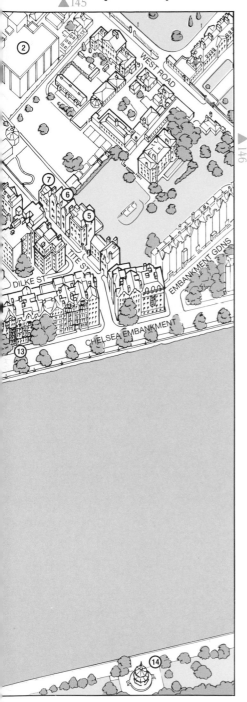

▲ 145

▶ 146

① **The Surprise**, popular 'local' with prints of old Chelsea on the walls. ② **National Army Museum**, purpose-built and opened in 1971. History of the British Army from Henry VII to the present day; models, dioramas, weapons, uniforms, paintings. ③ **La Tante Claire** (No. 68), Pierre Koffmann's summery, understated temple of modern French gastronomy (**£££**). ④ **Swan Walk**, cluster of graceful 18thC houses, set back. Walton's *Façade* was first performed in one, briefly inhabited by Edith Sitwell 1917-19. ⑤ In **Tite Street**, the scene of much artistic endeavour, No. 35, The White House (now replaced) was built by avant-garde architect Edward Godwin for Whistler (*see page 153*) in 1877, but he had to leave due to his libel case with Ruskin. ⑥ **No. 33**, Augustus John's studios. ⑦ **No. 31**, home of American artist John Singer Sargent, who died here. ⑧ **No. 34**, Oscar Wilde's marital home from 1884 to his arrest in 1895. It was suitably aesthetically decorated by Godwin (who also designed No. 44, The Tower House). ⑨ **Cheyne Walk**, elegant, much coveted single row of tall, mainly Queen Anne houses, built on the site of Henry VIII's Chelsea Manor, which was subsequently owned by the Cheyne and then the Sloane family. Until it became separated from the embankment, this was a bustling riverside street, which attracted a remarkable catalogue of famous residents (notable in modern times: Mick Jagger, Lord Weidenfeld, Paul Getty II, Gerald Scarfe) from artists, musicians and writers to eccentrics and misers (*see also pages 149 and 153*). ⑩ **No. 4** (fine ironwork and doorway) is where the elderly, newly married George Eliot died. ⑪ **Nos 7-11** date from the 1880s; David Lloyd George lived in No. 10. ⑫ **Chelsea Physic Garden** (open two afternoons in summer and during Chelsea Flower Show), botanical gardens established in 1673 by the Society of Apothecaries; exotic trees, shrubs and herbs. ⑬ Fine houses along this stretch of Chelsea Embankment (*see page 147*) include **Nos 18, 17, 15, 11, 10, 9 and 8** (notice the clock) by Richard Norman Shaw, leading exponent of the 'Queen Anne style' in London (c1870s), and **Nos 6, 5 and 4** by Godwin (conventional for him). ⑭ **London Peace Pagoda**, 1985, built in Battersea Park by Japanese Buddhist monks, a tranquil addition to the riverside.

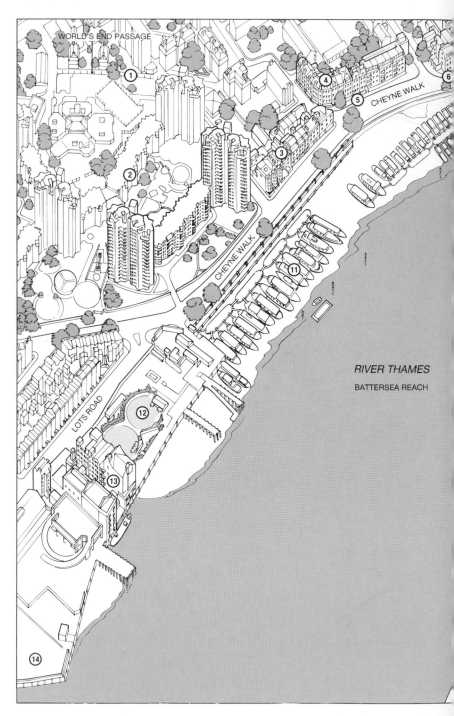

WORLD'S END PASSAGE

CHEYNE WALK

CHEYNE WALK

LOTS ROAD

RIVER THAMES

BATTERSEA REACH

Cheyne Walk/Lots Road

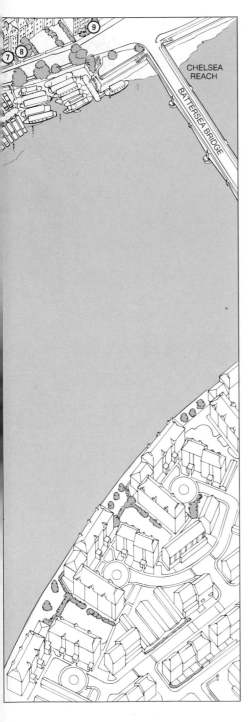

① **World's End Passage** once approached a 17thC inn bearing the same name, and a tea garden. It is now engulfed by a large housing estate which incorporates ② the **Chelsea Towers** complex. World's End is the western boundary of Chelsea. ③ At **119 Cheyne Walk** (*see also pages 149 and 151*) the eccentric and elderly J.M.W. Turner, found solitude and anonymity under the name of Booth. He died there in 1851. ④ **Ziani Dolce**, No. 112, a smart Italian restaurant (**££**), curves around Munroe Terrace. ⑤ **Nos 109** and **108** were the homes, earlier this century, of the painter Philip Wilson Steer and the sculptor John Tweed respectively. ⑥ Hilaire Belloc lived at **No. 104** between 1901 and 1905. ⑦ **No. 101** was the first of ten Chelsea addresses for the American painter Whistler. He called Chelsea 'the wonderful village', and stayed from 1862 until his death in 1903. ⑧ A cream-coloured country mansion, **Lindsey House**, Nos 96-100, is the only reminder of the days when Chelsea was known as a 'Town of Palaces' (Defoe). Built c1674 as the seat of the Earl of Lindsey, it was subdivided into five houses in the 1770s, and has embraced as residents Count Zinzendorf and his Moravian community (a failure), the engineers Brunel, father (Marc Isambard) and son (Isambard Kingdom) and Whistler (again). ⑨ **Nos 91-95** are notable: Nos 91 and 92 have attractive Venetian windows, and No. 91 a glazed first-floor veranda. Mrs Gaskell was born at No. 93 in 1810. ⑩ Bazalgette's 1880s wrought-iron **Battersea Bridge** replaced an earlier wooden one often depicted by Whistler. It links Battersea with Chelsea, at the point where Sir Thomas More's 16thC country estate once stood. ⑪ Gaily painted houseboats line the **Chelsea Basin**. ⑫ **Cremorne Gardens**, a welcome open space overlooking the river, commemorates the pleasure gardens which started life in 1832 as a sporting stadium (hence Stadium Street) and evolved into a delightful open-air centre of 19thC entertainments: balloon ascents, fireworks, pageants, grottoes and music. They closed in 1877 and today only an ornate iron entrance gate remains, now displayed in the present garden. ⑬ **Chelsea Wharf**, a flour mill converted to offices, studios, a sprinkling of shops and a Chinese restaurant, Dynasty, (**££**). Also the London Wine Co: wines by the case. ⑭ **Chelsea Harbour**, a yuppified, sanitized fantasy 'riverside village' development (completion 1990), built around a yacht basin beyond Chelsea Creek (off map).

153

RIVER THAMES
GREENWICH REACH
Greenwich Pier

Greenwich Footway Tunnel

CUTTY SARK GARDENS

Royal Naval College

COLLEGE APPROACH

GREENWICH CHURCH STREET

KING WILLIAM WALK

Greenwich Market

DURNFORD ST

ROMNEY ROAD

NELSON ROAD

STRAIGHTSMOUTH

STOCKWELL STREET

NEVADA ST

KING WILLIAM WALK

Greenwich

① Victorian-tiled **Greenwich Footway Tunnel**, linking Greenwich to the Isle of Dogs. ② Site of **Greenwich Palace**. Built in 1427 by Henry V's brother, the Duke of Gloucester, it was the scene of Tudor banquets, jousting tournaments and hunting parties. Wren demolished it to build the Royal Naval Hospital (now the Royal Naval College). ③ Marble **statue of George II** in Roman dress by J. M. Rysbrack (1735). ④ **King Charles's Quarters**, oldest part of the Royal Naval College, built in 1664 by John Webb (a pupil of Inigo Jones) as a wing of a new palace, which remained unfinished due to lack of funds. ⑤ Almost 30 years later, Queen Mary commissioned Wren to build a naval hospital. The hospital closed in 1869, and in 1873 the **Royal Naval College** moved here from Portsmouth. ⑥ **Queen Anne's Quarters** (1728), built by Vanbrugh, who succeeded Wren and used his plans, beneath which is the undercroft of Greenwich Palace. **Gipsy Moth IV** (off map), a 53ft ketch in which Sir Francis Chichester sailed solo around the world in 1966-7. ⑦ **Cutty Sark**, magnificent 19thC tea clipper, the fastest of its kind, has a display of historical documents and a wonderful collection of figureheads. ⑧ In Queen Mary's Quarter, Wren's **Chapel** was damaged by fire and restored with a delicate rococo interior by James 'Athenian' Stuart. ⑨ **Painted Hall** (1727) in King William's Quarter, where Sir James Thornhill's vast baroque paintings, celebrating Britain's Protestant monarchy, decorate the ceiling of Wren's domed building. ⑩ **Dreadnought Seamen's Hospital**, built by 'Athenian' Stuart in 1763. ⑪ **National Maritime Museum**, where exhibits range from decorated royal river boats to Turner paintings, is centred on ⑫ **Queen's House**, Inigo Jones's perfect Palladian villa. ⑬ **King's Arms**, pub with nautical prints and a pleasant garden. ⑭ Hawksmoor church, **St Alfege's** (1718), marks the site of the martyrdom of the Archbishop of Canterbury at the hands of the Danes in 1012. ⑮ **Greenwich Park**, the beautiful grounds of Greenwich Palace, added to the estate in 1433 and landscaped by Le Nôtre in Charles II's reign. ⑯ **Greenwich Theatre**, a 19thC music-hall, rebuilt in 1969. Other buildings of interest are the Old Royal Observatory and Flamsteed House, both by Wren, the Meridian Building and Ranger's House, both 18thC (all off map).

GENERAL POINTS OF INTEREST

A

Abbey National building 43
Abchurch Lane 99
Achilles, statue (Hyde Park) 103
Adam Street 89
Adelphi, The 89
Admiralty Arch 57, 109, 125
Albert Bridge 149
Albert Court 117
Albert Embankment 147
Albert Hall Mansions 117
Albert Memorial (Kensington Gardens) 117
Albion Wireworks 53
Aldersgate 55
Aldwych 69, 91
Amen Court 73
Annabel's Club 83
Antiques Fair 143
Apothecaries' Hall 73
Apsley House 103
Architectural Association 47
Argyll House 143
Arlington House 107
Athenaeum Hotel 109
Austin Friars 77
Australia House 69

B

Bank of England 77
Bankside 97
Banqueting House (Whitehall) 111
Barbican, The 55
Barbican Arts & Conference Centre 55
Basinghall Street 77
Battersea Bridge 153
Battersea Park 151
Baynard House 95
Baynard's Castle site 95
Bayswater Road 57
Beak Street 63
Bear Gardens 97
Beauchamp Place 131
Beaver House 97
Bedford Estate 47
Bedford Place 47
Bedford Row 49
Beefeaters/Yeomen of the Guard 115
Belgrave Mews West 121
Belgrave Square 121
Belgravia 119, 121, 137
Belvedere Road 113
Berkeley Square 83
Berwick Street 65
Big Ben 129
Birdcage Walk 127
Birkbeck College 47
Blackfriars Bridge 95
Blackfriars railway bridges 95
Blackfriars Station 95
Blewcoat School site 125

Blomfield Road 45
Bloomsbury 47
Boating Lake (Regent's Park) 43
Boltons, The 141
Bond Street 61
Boodle's Club 107
Booth's Gin Distillery 53
Bousfield Primary School 141
Bow Street 67
Bow Street Courts 67
Bowater House 119
Bracken House 75
Bread Street 75
Brewer Street 65
Brewers' Hall 55
Bridewell Place 73
Bridewell Prison site 73
Bridgewater Square 55
British Academy 43
British Library 47
Broad Court 67
Broad Sanctuary 127
Broad Walk (Kensington Gardens) 101
Broad Walk (Regent's Park) 41
Broadway House 127
Brompton Road 131
Brompton Square 131
Brooke Street 51
Brooks's Club 107
Bruton Street 83
Buckingham Palace 57, 109, 121, 123, 125
Buckingham Palace Road 139
Buckingham Street 89
Burlington Arcade 85
Burlington Estate 85
Burlington House 85
Burton's Court 145
Bush House 69

C

Cabinet Office 111
Cabinet War Rooms 127
cabman's shelter 61
Cadogan Estate 137, 149
Cadogan Place 137
Cadogan Square 137
Caledonian Club 121
Caledonian Market 79
Cambridge Circus 65
Camden 41
Campden Hill Road 79
Canada House 87
canal towpaths 45
Cannon Street 99
Cannon Street Station 99
Carey Street 71
Carlton Club 107
Carlton House 63, 109
Carlton House Terrace 109
Carlyle Square 149
Carmelite Street 93
Carnaby Street 63
Carter Lane 73

Cavalry & Guards Club 105
Cavendish Square 61
Cecil Court 89
Cenotaph (Whitehall) 111
Central School of Art & Design, The 49
Chancery Lane 71
Charing Cross 89
Charing Cross Road 65
Charterhouse 53
Cheapside 75
Chelsea 119, 137
Chelsea Barracks 147
Chelsea Basin 153
Chelsea Embankment 147, 151
Chelsea Flower Show 147, 151
Chelsea Green 143
Chelsea Harbour 153
Chelsea Old Town Hall 143
Chelsea Physic Garden 151
Chelsea School of Art 143
Chelsea Towers 153
Chelsea Wharf 153
Cheltenham Terrace 145
Chepstow Villas 79
Chesterfield Street 105
Cheyne Row 149
Cheyne Walk 149, 151, 153
Chinatown 65, 87
Christie's 107
Church House 127
churches
    All Hallows-by-the-Tower 115
    of the Annunciation 57
    Chapel Royal 107
    Chelsea Old Church 149
    Christ Church Greyfriars 73
    French Protestant 65
    Grosvenor Chapel 81
    Guards Chapel 127
    Holy Trinity (Brompton Road) 131
    Holy Trinity (Sloane Street) 137
    Immaculate Conception (RC) 83
    Methodist Central Hall 127
    Nôtre Dame de France (RC) 87
    Oratory (RC) 131
    Queen's Chapel, The 107
    Rolls Chapel site 71
    St Alban the Martyr 51
    St Alfege's Greenwich 155
    St Andrew 51
    St Andrew-by-the-Wardrobe 95
    St Anne and St Agnes 75
    St Bartholomew the Great 53
    St Benet 95
    St Bride 73
    St Clement Danes 69
    St Clement's Eastcheap 99
    St Dunstan-in-the-West 71
    St Edmund the King 77
    St Etheldreda (RC) 51
    St George's (Bond Street) 61
    St George's (Hanover Square) 81
    St Giles Cripplegate 55

    St James Garlickhithe 97
    St James's (Piccadilly) 85
    St Lawrence Jewry 75
    St Luke's 143
    St Magnus 99
    St Margaret Lothbury 77
    St Margaret's Westminster 129
    St Martin Ludgate 73
    St Martin-in-the-Fields 89
    St Mary Abbots 101
    St Mary Abchurch 99
    St Mary Aldermary 75
    St Mary-le-Bow 75
    St Mary-le-Strand 91
    St Mary-the-Boltons 141
    St Mary Woolnoth 77
    St Marylebone 43
    St Michael 77
    St Michael Paternoster Royal 97
    St Nicholas Cole Abbey 97
    St Paul's (Covent Garden) 67
    St Paul's Knightsbridge 121
    St Peter (Cornhill) 77
    St Peter's 61
    St Sepulchre 73
    St Stephen Wallbrook 77
    St Thomas More 149
    St Vedast-alias-Foster 75
    St Paul's Cathedral 73, 75
    Savoy Chapel, The 91
    Temple Church 71
    Ukrainian Catholic Cathedral 59
    Westminster Abbey 89, 129
    Westminster Cathedral 139
cinemas
    Coronet 79
    Curzon 105
    Gate 79
    Odeon 57
Citadel, The 109
City Club 77
City of London boundary 93
City of London School for Boys 95
City of London School for Girls 55
Clarence House 107
Clarence Terrace 42
Cleopatra's Needle 91
Clermont Club 83
Clifton Little Venice 45
Clifton Nurseries 45
Clifton Villas 45
Cockpit Stairs 127
Cockpit Yard 49
College Hill 97
College of Arms 97
College of St Spirit & St Mary site 97
concert halls
    Conway 49
    Purcell Room 113
    Queen Elizabeth 113
    Royal Festival 113
Connaught Square 57
Constable Collection (Victoria & Albert

Museum 133
Constitution Arch 57, 121
Constitution Hill 123
Cork Street 75
Cornwall Terrace 43
Courtauld Institute 91
Covent Garden 47
Covent Garden Central Market 67
Craft Concert Gallery 87
Craig's Court 111
Cremorne Gardens 153
Crewe House 105
Crimean War Memorial 87
Cripplegate site 55
Crockfords Club 105
Crosby Hall 149
Crown Jewels 115
Crown office Row 93
Curzon Street 105
Cutty Sark 155

D

Daily Express building 73
David, statue (Hyde Park Corner) 103
Davies Mews 61
Davies Street 61
Dean Street 65
Dean's Yard 127
Delamere Terrace 45
Department of Trade & Industry 127
Design Centre 87
Devereux Court 93
Distaff Lane 97
Docklands 71
Domesday Book (Public
    Record Office Museum) 71
Dowgate Hill 99
Downing Street 111
Dreadnought Seamen's Hospital 155
Drury Lane 69
Dudley House 81
Duke of York's 145
Duke of York's Column 109
Duke Street 59
Dyers' Hall 99

E

Eastcheap 99
Eaton Square 137
Eaton Terrace Mews 137
Economist Building 107
Edgware Road 57
Egerton Crescent 135
Elgin Marbles (British Museum) 47
Ely Place 51
Emerson Street 97
English National Opera 89
English Stage Company 137
Ennismore Street 131
Eros 87
Essex Street 93

F

Faraday Building 95
Farringdon Station 53
Farringdon Street 53, 95
Festival of Britain (1951) 113
Fish Street Hill 99
Fishmongers' Hall 99
Flamstead House (Greenwich) 155
Fleet Prison site 73
Fleet River 73, 95
Fleet Street 71
Frederick's Place 77
French Embassy 119
Friday Street 75
Frith Street 65

G

Garrick Club 67
Gatwick 139
Gees Court 59
Gelding's Close site 63
Gerrard Place 65
Gerrard Street 65
Gilston Street 141
Gipsy Moth IV 155
Gledhow Street 141
Golden Lane 55
Golden Square 63
Goldsmith Street 75
Goldsmiths' Hall 75
Goodrich Court 97
Goodwins Court 89
Gough Square 71
Gower Street 47
Gracechurch Street 97
Grand Union Canal 41, 45
Gray's Inn 49, 51
Gray's Inn Gardens 51
Gray's Inn Hall 51
Gray's Inn Road 51
Gray's Inn Square 51
Great Exhibition (1851) 117, 131
Great Fire of London (1666)
    73, 75, 95, 97, 99, 111
Great James Street 49
Great Marlborough Street 63
Great Russell Street 47
Great Turnstile 49
Greek Street 65
Green Park 105, 107
Green Street 59
Greenwich 155
Greenwich Footway Tunnel 155
Greenwich Palace site 155
Greenwich Park 155
Grosvenor Estate 59, 81, 83, 121
Grosvenor Gardens 123
Grosvenor Square 81
Guard, changing of the 125
Guildhall 75
Guildhall Library 75
Guildhall School of Music & Drama 55
Guinness World of Records Exhibition 87

Gunter Estate 141
Gwydyr House 111

H

HMS Wellington 93
Half Moon Street 105
Halkin Arcade 121
Hampton Court 137
Hanover Square 61, 81
Harrow Road 45
Hatton Garden 51
Haymarket 87
Hayward Gallery 113
Henry Cole Wing
        (Victoria & Albert Museum) 133
High Holborn 49
Hobart House 123
Holborn 51, 53
Holborn Bars 51
Holborn Viaduct 53
Home House 59
Home Office 127
Horse Guards 111
Hospital of St Katharine site 115
hotels
  Athenaeum 105
  Basil Street 119
  Berkeley 121
  Blakes 141
  Britannia, The 81
  Brown's 85
  Capital, The 119
  Cavendish 85
  Claridge's 61
  Connaught, The 83
  Cumberland, The 57
  Dorchester, The 103
  Duke's 107
  Fenja 137
  Fielding, The 67
  Goring, The 139
  Grosvenor, The 139
  Grosvenor House 81
  Hazlitt's 65
  Hilton, The 103
  Howard 91
  Hyatt Carlton Tower 119
  Hyde Park 119
  Inn on the Park, The 103
  Inter-Continental, The 103
  L'Hotel 119
  London Marriott 59
  Londonderry, The 103
  Mayfair, The 83
  Meridien 85
  Mount Royal 59
  Park Lane 105
  Piccadilly 85
  Rembrandt, The 131
  Royal Garden 101
  Royal Horseguards 111
  Royal Westminster 139
  Russell 47

  St James's Court 125
  Savoy, The 91
  Selfridge 59
  Sheraton Park Tower 119
  Stafford 107
  Stakis St Ermin's 127
  Strand Palace, The 91
  Tower Thistle 115
  Waldorf 69, 91
  Westbury 83
  Wilbrahim, The 137
House of Commons 129
House of Lords 129
Hudson's Bay Company 97
Huggin Hill 97
Hungerford Bridge (rail) 111
Hyde Park 103
Hyde Park Barracks 119
Hyde Park Corner 57, 103, 121
Hyde Park Estate 57
Hyde Park Place 57

I

Imperial College of Science & Technology 117
Information Centre, City
        (St Paul's Church Yard) 75
Inner Temple 93
Inner Temple Garden 93
Inner Temple Hall 71
Inner Temple Library 71
Innholders' Hall 99
Institute of Chartered Accountants, The 79
Institute of Contemporary Art 109
Institute of Directors 109
Isle of Dogs 155
Ismaili Centre 133

J

Jason's Trip 45
Jermyn Street 85
Jewel Tower (Westminster) 129
John Street 49
John Adam Street 89
John Carpenter Street 95
Jubilee Hall 67
Junior Carlton Club 109
Juxon House 73

K

Kensington Church Street 79, 101
Kensington Gardens 101, 103, 117
Kensington Gravel Pits site 79
Kensington High Street 101
Kensington Palace 101, 145
Kensington Palace Gardens 101
Kensington Park Road 79
King Charles Street 127
King Street St James's 107
King William Street 99
King's Bench Walk 93
King's College 91
King's Road 137, 143, 145
King's Troop, Royal Horse Artillery 57

Kingsway 69, 91
Kinnerton Street 121
Knightsbridge 119, 137
Knightsbridge Green 119

L

Ladbroke Estate 79
Ladbroke Grove 79
Lamb Buildings 93
Lamb's Conduit Street 49
Lancaster House 107
Law Courts/Royal Courts of Justice 69, 71
Law Society 71
Lawrence Street 149
Leather Lane 51
Lees Place 59
Leicester Square 87
Les Ambassadeurs Club 103
Lincoln's Inn 69
Lincoln's Inn Chapel 71
Lincoln's Inn Fields 49, 69
Lindow Man (British Museum) 47
Lindsey House (Cheyne Walk) 153
Lindsey House (Lincoln's Inn Fields) 69
Lisle Street 87
Little Dean's Yard 129
Little Venice 41, 45
Lombard Street 77, 99
London Bridge 99
London Library 85
London Pavilion 87
London Peace Pagoda 151
London Salvage Corps 55
London School of
    Economics & Political Science 69
London School of
    Hygiene & Tropical Medicine 47
London Stone, The 99
London Symphony Orchestra 55
London Transport headquarters 127
London University 47, 69, 91, 117
London Waterbus Company 45
Lowndes Square 119
Ludgate 71
Lycurgus Cup (British Museum) 47

M

Madame Tussauds 43
Maida Avenue 45
Malet Street 47
Mall, The 109, 125
Mall Galleries 109
Manchester Square 59
Mansion House 77
Marble Arch 57
Markham Square 145
Marlborough House 107
Master Mariners' Livery Hall 93
Mayfair 121
Mercantile Marine Memorial 115
Meridian Building (Greenwich) 155
Metropolitan Police headquarters 127
Michelin House 135

Middle Temple 93
Middle Temple Gardens 93
Middle Temple Hall 93
Middle Temple Library 93
Midland Bank (Poultry) 77
Mildenhall Treasure (British Museum) 47
Milk Street 75
Ministry of Defence 111
Montpelier Street 131
Monument, The 99
Morpeth Terrace 139
Motcomb Street 121
Mount Row 83
Mount Street 81, 83
Munroe Terrace 153
museums
    British 47, 85, 133
    Clockmakers' Company 75
    Geological 133
    Guards 125
    India 133
    London Transport 67
    of London 55
    of Mankind 85
    of the Moving Image 113
    National Army 151
    National Maritime 155
    Natural History 133
    Postal Museum 75
    Public Record Office 71
    Science 133
    Shakespeare Globe 97
    Sikorski 117
    Soane 69
    Theatre 67
    Victoria & Albert 131, 133

N

Wellington 103
National Gallery 87
National Portrait Gallery 87
National Sound Archive 117
National Theatre 113
National Theatre Company 113
National Trust Shop
    & Information Centre 125
National Westminster Bank
    (High Holborn) 49
Naval & Military Club 105
Neal's Yard 67
New Bond Street 61
New Ministry of Defence 111
New Scotland Yard 127
New Turnstile 49
New Zealand House 87
Newgate Prison site 57, 73
Norman Shaw Building 129
North Audley Street 59
Notting Hill Carnival 79
Notting Hill Gate 79

O

Oakley Street 149

Ognisko Polskie/Polish Hearth Club 117
Old Admiralty III
Old Bailey 73
Old Bond Street 85
Old Brompton Road 141
Old Burlington Street 88
Old Church Street 149
Old Compton Street 65
Old Jewry 77
Old London Bridge site 99
Old Queen Street 127
Old Royal Observatory (Greenwich) 155
Orangery (Kensington Gardens) 101
Oriental Club 61
Outer Circle (Regent's Park) 41
Oxenden Street 87
Oxford & Cambridge Club 107
Oxford Circus 63
Oxford Street 57, 61, 65

P

Painted Hall (Royal Naval College) 155
Palace Green (Kensington Palace) 101
Palace of Westminster site 129
Palace of Whitehall site 111
Pall Mall 107, 109
Palladium House 63
Pantechnicon, The 121
Pantheon site 63
Parade, The (Horse Guards) 111
Park Lane 81, 103
Parliament, Houses of 129
Parliament Square 129
Passport Office 125
Paternoster Square 73
Pearl Assurance building 49
Pelham Crescent 135
Pembridge Crescent 79
Pembridge Square 79
Pembridge Villas 79
Petty France 125
Piazza, The (Covent Garden) 67
Piccadilly 85, 105
Piccadilly Circus 87
Pimlico 121, 137
Pirelli Garden
     (Victoria & Albert Museum) 133
Planetarium, The 43
Plowden Buildings 93
Polish Hearth Club/Ognisko Polskie 117
Pond Place 135
Portman Square 59
Portobello Road 79
Portpool Lane 51
Portugal Street 69
Post Office 75, 123
Postman's Park 75
Princes Gardens 117
Princes Gate 117
Printing House Square 95
Priory Street 141
Prudential Assurance building 51
public houses & wine bars

Admiral Codrington 135
Antelope, The 137
Bar Italia 65
Blackfriar, The 95
Bow Wine Vault 75
Brinkley's Champagne Bar 105
Bunch of Grapes, The 131
Castle, The 53
Cheshire Cheese, The 93
Cittie of York 51
Coach & Horses 63
Edgar Wallace 93
El Vino 71
Ennismore Arms 131
Fox & Anchor, The 53
Grenadier, The 121
Grove Travern 131
Guinea, The 83
Henekey's Wine Bar 49
Jimmie's Wine Bar 101
King's Arms 155
King's Head & Eight Bells 149
Lamb & Flag, The 67
Museum Tavern 47
Nag's Head 121
Old Bell Inn 73
Phené Arms 149
Pontefract Castle, The 59
Prince Albert 79
Printer's Devil 71
Punch Tavern 73
Red Lion, The 83
Salisbury, The 89
Samuel Pepys 97
Ship Tavern, The 69
Silver Cross 111
Square Rigger, The 99
Star Tavern 121
Sun in Splendour 79
Surprise, The 151
Tiger Tavern 115
Turk's Head 121
Two Chairmen 127
Viaduct Tavern 73
Warwick Castle, The 45
Westminster Arms 127
White House 71
White Swan, The 93
Whittington's 97
Witness Box, The 93
Ye Olde Cheshire Cheese 71
Ye Olde Cock Tavern 71
Ye Old Mitre 51
Yorkshire Grey, The 49
Public Record Office 71
Pudding Lane 99
Punch 73

Q

Quadrant (Regent Street) 63
Queen Anne's Gate 127
Queen Anne's Mews 127
Queen Mary's Rose Gardens (Regent's Park) 43

Queen Mary's Steps 111
Queen Street 97
Queen's Gallery, The 125
Queen's House (Greenwich) 155
Queen's Tower 133
Queenhithe 97

R

Ranelagh Gardens site 147
Ranelagh House site 147
Ranger's House (Greenwich) 155
Raphael Cartoons
    (Victoria & Albert Museum) 133
Red Lion Square 49
Reform Club 109
Regent Street 63, 109
Regent's Canal 41, 45
Regent's Park 42, 45, 63, 109
restaurants and/or cafés
    Al Hamra 105
    Al-Madina 57
    Al Sultan 105
    Alexander's 145
    Allen's, Joe 91
    Andronicas Coffee Shop 101
    Bahn Thai 65
    Bean's, Henry J. 143
    Bentley's 85
    Bibendum 135
    Bishop's Finger 53
    Blank's, Justin de 59
    Boswell's Coffee House 67
    Boulestin 67
    Bumbles 139
    Café Casbar 67
    Café Royal 85
    Calabash, The 67
    Carriages 139
    Chuen Cheng Ku 87
    Cranks 63
    Dan's 143
    Daquise 133
    Dragon Gate 65
    Drakes 135
    Drury Tea & Coffee Co 113
    Dynasty 153
    Edmunds, Andrew 63
    Fayrouz 59
    Fifty-one Fifty-one 135
    French House, The 65
    Fridays 89
    Fung Shing 87
    Galleon, The 79
    Gay Hussar 65
    Geales 79
    Greenhouse, The 83
    Grouse & Claret, The 123
    Guinea Grill 83
    Hard Rock Café 105
    Harry's 63
    Ikeda 61, 83
    Institute of Contemporary Arts 109
    Jimmy's 65

Jones, Inigo 67
Jones, Maggie 101
L'Auberge de Provence 125
L'Escargot
La Brasserie 135
La Tante Claire 151
Langan's 105
Le Café du Marché 53
Le Caprice 107
Le Gamin 73
Le Gavroche 81
Le Métro 119
Le Poulbot 75
Le Suguet 135
Luba's Bistro 131
Little, Alastair 65
London Chinatown 65
Luigi's 91
Ma Cuisine 135
Maison Bertaux 65
Manzi's 87
Maroush 57
Mélange 67
Ménage à Trois 131
Meridiana 135
Miyama 105
Mon Plaisir 67
Monkeys 143
Mr Chow 119
New Diamond 87
New World 65
One Two Three 83
Oriel 137
Orso 91
Overtons 139
Paper Tiger 133
Pheasantry, The 143
'Pier 31' 149
Pizza Expresss 65
Pontack's 99
Poons 87
Porters 89
Punters 99
Quo Vadis 65
Read's 141
Red Fort 65
Richoux 119
Ritz, The 107
Rules 89
St Quentin 131
Salloos 121
San Lorenzo 131
Savvas Kebab House 79
Shampers 63
Simpson's-in-the-Strand 91
Smithfield Ale & Chop House 53
Stockpot, The 119
Straits 105
Sweetings 75
Tiddy Dols 105
Villa Claudius 127
Widow Applebaum's Wine Bar 61
Zen 135

Zen Central 83
Ziani Dolce 153
Reuters 73
Riding House, The 123
Robert Street 89
'Roman bath' 91
Roper's Gardens 149
Rosary Gardens 141
Rosetta Stone (British Museum) 47
Rotten Row (Hyde Park) 119
Round Pond (Kensington Gardens) 101
Royal Albert Hall 117, 133
Royal Academy of Arts 85
    Summer Exhibition 85
Royal Artillery Monument 121
Royal Automobile Club 109
Royal Avenue 145
Royal Cockpit site 127
Royal College of Music 117
Royal College of Organists 117
Royal College of Surgeons 69
Royal Courts of Justice/Law Courts 69, 71
Royal Exchange 77
Royal Geographical Society 117
Royal Horse Artillery 57
Royal Hospital 145
Royal Hospital Burial Ground 147
Royal Hospital grounds 147
Royal Hospital Road 147
Royal Institution, The 83, 85
Royal Mews 123
Royal Naval College 155
    King Charles Quarters 155
    King William's Quarter 155
    Queen Anne's Quarters 155
    Queen Mary's Quarter 155
Royal Naval Hospital 155
Royal Opera Arcade 87
Royal Opera House 67
Royal Shakespeare Theatre Co 55, 69

S

Saffron Hill 51
St Alban's church tower 75
St Alphage Garden 55
St Barnabas, House of 65
St Bartholomew's Hospital 53
St Christopher's Place 59
St George Street 61
St George's Hospital site 121
St James's 107, 109
St James's Palace 107
St James's Park 109, 127
St James's Square 109
St James's Street 107
St John's Street 53
St Katharine's Dock 115
St Leonard's Terrace 145
St Olave Jewry church tower 77
Salisbury Court 73
Salters' Hall 55
Salvation Army International HQ 97
Sanctuary Tower site 127

Savile Club 61
Savile Row 85
Schomberg House 107
School of Mines 117
School of Oriental & African Studies 47
Scott's, Ronnie, Club 65
sculptures & statues 41, 47, 49, 51, 55, 61,
    63, 67, 69, 71, 73, 87, 89, 95, 97, 101,
    103, 107, 115, 117, 119, 125, 127, 129,
    139, 143, 147, 149, 155
Senate House (London University) 47
Serpentine, The 103
Seven Dials 67
Shaftesbury Avenue 65
Shell Centre 113
Shell-Mex House 89, 91
Shepherd Market 105
shops & stores
    HMSO Bookshop 49
    Agnes B 135
    Allans 59
    Allen, J. A. 139
    Amies, Hardy 85
    Antiquarius 143
    Armani, Giorgio 61
    Ashley, Laura 135
    Asprey 61, 85
    Bailey, John & Sons 83
    Barclay, Jack 83
    Beauchamp Place Shop 131
    Bell, John & Croyden 59
    Bendicks 59
    Berry Bros & Rudd 107
    Berwick Street Market 65
    Bonhams 131
    Bonsack 81
    Bourdon House 83
    Brown's 61
    Brumfit, John 53
    Burberry's 87
    Burke, John & Partners 79
    Camisa 65
    Chanel 85
    Charbonnel et Walker 85
    Charles, Caroline 131
    Chelsea Antique Market 149
    Chelsea Design Co, The 143
    Chelsea Gardner, The 143
    Chelsea Kitchen 145
    Chenil Galleries, The 143
    Chicago Pizza Pie Factory 61
    Churchill, Jane 137
    Coles 137
    Conran 135
    Costa Coffee Boutique 139
    Counter Spy Shop 81
    Crabtree & Evelyn 101
    Craftsmen Potters Shop 63
    Debenham 61
    Dickens's Old Curiosity Shop 69
    Dickins & Jones 63
    Divertimenti 135
    Ede & Ravenscroft 71

English Eccentrics 135
Fenwick's 61
Ferragamo 85
Fielden, David 143
Fortnum & Mason 85
General Trading Co, The 137
Gieves & Hawkes 85
Goode, Thomas, & Co 81
Gray's Market 61
Grey House Books 149
Gucci 85
Hamleys 63
Harrods 59, 119, 131
Hatchard's 85
Higgins, H. R. 59
Hobbs 81
Holland & Holland 83
House of Hardy 107
Hyper Hyper 101
Jones, Peter 137
Kensington Market 101
Lewis, John 61, 137
Liberty 63
Lobb's 107
Lock, James & Co 107
London Silver Vaults 53
Mappin & Webb 77
Marks & Spencer 63
Nelson, A. & Co 59
Nichols, Harvey 119
Nutter, Tommy 85
Oldfield, Bruce 131
Oliver, John 79
Packer, Jane 59
Paperchase 87
Partridges 137
Patisserie Valerie 65
Paxton & Whitfield 85
Portobello Road Street Market 79
Purdey, James & Co 81
Reger, Janet 131
Rhodes, Zandra 83
Richards 65
Ronay, Edina 143
Russian Shop, The 53
Sandoe, John 137
Scotch House 119
Selfridges 59
Simpsons 85
Sleeping Company, The 135
Smallbone of Devizes 135
Smith, H. Allan 149
Sotheby's 61
Spink & Co 107
Stanford, Edward 67
Transalpino 139
Trumper, George F. 105
Twining, R. & Co 71
Wells, Mother 99
Westaway & Westaway 47
Skinners Hal 99
Sloane Square 137
Sloane Street 119, 137

Smith's Charity Estate 135, 143
Smithfield Central Markets 53
Snow Hill 53
Society of Apothecaries 151
Society of Authors 141
Soho 65
Soho Square 65
Somerset House 91
Soper Lane site 97
Sotheby's 61
South Audley Street 81
South Bank Arts Centre 113
South Bank Craft Centre 113
South Molton Street 61
Southampton House site 47
Southwark Bridge 97
Speaker's Corner (Hyde Park) 57
Stadium Street 153
Stag Brewery site 139
Staple Inn 51
State Coaches (Royal Mews) 123
State House 49
Stationers' Hall 73
Stew Lane 97
Stock Exchange 77
Strand, The 89, 91
Stratford Place 61
Suffolk Place 87
Suffolk Street 87
Suffragette Memorial 127
Sutton Hoo Treasure (British Museum)
Swan Uppers 93
Swan Walk 151
Sydney Street 143
Symons Street 137

T

Tallow Chandlers' Hall 99
Tedworth Square 145
Telecom Technology Showcase 95
Temple Bar 71
Temple of Mithras remains 77
Temple Stairs 93
Terminus Place 139
Thames River trips 129
theatres
    Aldwych 69, 91
    Apollo Victoria 139
    Coliseum, The 89
    Cottesloe (National Theatre) 113
    Criterion 87
    Donmar Warehouse 67
    Fortune (former) 55
    Gate Theatre Club 79
    Gaumont site 79
    Globe (replica) 97
    Greenwich 155
    Her Majesty's 87
    Jeannetta Cochrane 49
    London Palladium 63
    Lyceum, The 91
    Lyttleton (National Theatre) 113
    Mermaid, The 95

National Film 113
Olivier (National Theatre) 113
Palace 65
Royal Court 137
Royalty 69
Savoy, The 91
Strand, The 91
Theatre Royal Drury Lane 69
Theatre Royal Haymarket 87
Victoria Palace 139
Theobald's Road 49
Thurloe Square 135
Times, The 95
Tite Street 151
Torrington Square 47
Tower Bridge 115
Tower Green 115
Tower Hill 115
Tower of London 115
　Beauchamp Tower 115
　Bloody Tower 115
　Queen's House 115
　Traitors' Gate 115
　Waterloo Barracks 115
　White Tower 115
Tower Place 115
Tower Royal 97
Tratalgar Square 89
Travellers' Club 109
Tregunter Road 141
Trevor Square 131
Trocadero 87
Trooping the Colour 111
Turnagain Lane 73
Turnmill Street 53
Tyburn Convent 57
Tyburn, River 43

U

US Embassy 81
Unilever House 95
Upper Brook Street 81
Upper Cheyne Row 149
Uxbridge Street 79
Uxbridge Turnpike Trust 79

V

Verulam Buildings 51
Victoria Embankment 95, 111, 147
Victoria Embankment Gardens 111
Victoria Memorial 125
Victoria Square 139
Victoria Station 139
Victoria Street 139
Vintners' Hall 97

W

Wallace Collection 59
Walton Street 135
Warwick Avenue 45
Warwick Crescent 45
Watergate 95
Waterloo Bridge 113

Waterloo Place 109
Waterlo Vas (Buckingham Palace grounds)
　123
Wellington Barracks 125, 127
Wellington Square 145
Westminster 139
Westminster Abbey Choir School 127
Westminster Abbey Gardens 129
Westminster Bridge 129
Westminster Hall 129
Westminster, New Palace 129
Westminster Pier 129
Westminster School 129
Westway 45
Whitbread's Brewery 55
White's Club 85
Whitefriars Priory site 71
Whitehall 111, 129
Wilton Crescent 121
Wilton Street 123
Wood Street 75
World Trade Centre 115
World's End 143, 153
World's End Passage 153

Y

Yeomen of the Guard/Beefeaters 115
York Terrace 43
York Water Gate 89

Z

Zimbabwe House 89
Zoological Gardens 40-1, 45
Zoological Society of London 41

PEOPLE OF INTEREST

A

Abingdon, Abbot of 101
Abraham, H. R. 139
Adam, John & Robert
　59, 77, 89, 103, 105, 111
Albert, Prince 117
　statue, Holborn Circus 53
　statue, Kensington Gardens 117
Alexandra, Queen 107
Alfred, King 69
Allan, Godfrey 55
Allison, Sir Richard 133
Anne, Queen 101
　statue, Queen Anne's Gate 127
　statue, St Paul's Church Yard 73
Astafieva, Princess 143
Army & Navy Club 107
Arne, Thomas 149
Asquith, Herbert Henry 61
Audley, Sir Hugh 59
Avenant, Sir William d' 69

B

Bacon, Charles 51
Bacon, Francis 51
Baird, John Logie 65
Baker, Sir Herbert 77
Barbon, Nicholas 49, 93
Barry, Sir Charles 69, 89, 109, 129
Barry, E. M. 67, 87
Basevi, George 121, 135
Baucke, Heinrich 101
Bazalgette, Sir Joseph 111, 147
Beak, Thomas 63
Bedford, Earl of 67
Belcher, John 41, 77
Belloc, Hilaire 153
Bentley, J. F. 139
Bernhardt, Sarah 79
Besant, William 141
Birkbeck, Dr George 47
Blake, William 61
Boehm, Sir Joseph Edgar 103
Boleyn, Anne 115
Bonaparte, Napoleon 103, 113, 123
Bond, James 145
Boswell, James 67, 105
Boudicca, Queen, statue,
        Westminster Bridge 129
Bridgewater, Earls of 55
Brock, Sir Thomas 125
Browning, Elizabeth Barrett 43
Browning, Robert 43, 45
Brummel, Beau 105
Brunel, Isambard Kingdom 45, 153
Brunel, Marc Isambard 153
Brydon, John 143
Buckingham, Duke of 125
Burgoyne, General 105
Burne-Jones, Sir Edward 49, 137
Burton, Decimus 41, 43, 103, 109, 121
Burton, James 47
Butterfield, William 51
Byron, Lord 43

C

Cadogan, Elizabeth, Baroness Oakley 137
Campbell, Mrs Patrick 145
Canova 103, 113
Carlyle, Thomas 85, 145, 149
Carpenter, John 95
Casson, Sir Hugh 41, 133
Cavendish family 61
Cavendish, Lord 85
Caxton 71
Chamberlain, Powell & Bon 55
Chambers, Sir William 91
Chancellor of the Exchequer 111
Chantrey, Sir Francis Legatt 61
Charles I 111
        statue, Charing Cross 89
Charles II 103, 109, 111, 127, 137, 145, 155
        statue, Royal Hospital grounds 147
Charlotte, Queen 125

Chatterton, Thomas 51
Chichester, Sir Francis 155
Churchill, Winston 127
        statue, Parliament Square 129
Clive, Robert, statue, King Charles Street 127
Cockerell, Charles 147
Cocteau, Jean 87
Cole, Henry 133
Collins, Wilkie 43
Conran, Terence 135
Crewe, Bertie 69
Cromwell, Oliver 103
Cubitt, Joseph 95
Cubitt, Thomas 119, 121

D

Dance the Elder, George 77
Davy, Humphrey 83
Defoe, Daniel 153
Devereux, Robert, Earl of Essex 93
Dickens, Charles 51, 69, 143
Disraeli, Benjamin 49, 81, 103
Doll, Charles Fitzroy 47
Donaldson, T. L. 131

E

Edmund the Martyr 55
Edward the Confessor 129
Edward I 77, 89, 93, 95
        statue 49
Edward III 97
Edward VII 85
        statue 49
Eisenhower, Dwight G. 81
Eleanor, Queen 89
Eliot, George 151
Eliot, T. S. 49
Elizabeth I, Queen 51, 115, 125, 149
        statue 71
Elizabeth II, Queen 83, 123
Elizabeth, Queen Mother 83, 107
Epstein, Jacob 89, 119, 127
Evelyn, John 101

F

Fairbanks Jnr, Douglas 141
Faraday, Michael 83
Farrell, Terry 113
Fawkes, Guy 71
Fielding, Henry 67
Foch, Marshall, statue 139
Forster, E. M. 141
Fowke & Scott 117

G

Gainsborough 107
Galsworthy, John 141
Garb, Richard 49
Gaskell, Mrs 153
George II 101
        statue, Greenwich 155
George III 109, 123, 125
George IV 53, 109, 125

George, Sir Ernest 97
Getty II, Paul 151
Gibbons, Grinling 99, 101, 115, 147
Gibbons, Walter 63
Gibbs, James 53, 61, 69, 89, 91
Gilbert, Sir Alfred 107
Gill, Eric 127, 139
Gladstone, William Ewart, statue,
    Strand 69
Gloucester, Duke of 155
Godwin, Edward 151
Godwin, George 141
Gosse, Sir Edmund 45
Gray, Henry 123
Gresham, Sir Thomas 77
Grey, Reginald le 51
Gribble, Herbert 131
Grosvenor, 2nd Earl 121
Gwynn, Nell 107

H

Hamilton, Lady 43, 95
Handel, George Frederick 61
Hardwick, Philip 77
Hardwick, Thomas 43
Hatton, Christopher 51
Hawksmoor, Nicholas 77, 101, 155
Hawkshaw, Sir John 99
Hazlitt, William 65, 105
Henry I 53
Henry III 71, 115, 129
Henry V 155
Henry VII 129
Henry VIII 73, 103, 107, 111, 129, 149, 151
Hepworth, Barbara 49
Heywood, William 53
Hiseland, William 147
Hogarth, William 69
Holbein, Hans 149
Holden, Charles 47, 71
Holland, Henry 69
Holmes, Sherlock 43
Hood, Raymond 63
Howard, Thomas, Duke of Norfolk 53
Howell, James 55
Hudson, George 119
Hunt, James Henry Leigh 117, 149
Hunter, John 69

I

Irving, Henry 91

J

Jaeger, C. S. 121
Jagger, Mick 151
Jahangir, Sir Cowasjee 41
James I 111
James, John 61
Jenkins, W. K. 79
Joass, J. J. 41, 43
John, Augustus 151
Johnson, Samuel 67, 71, 93
Jones, Adrian 121

Jones, Sir Horace 53, 71, 115
Jones, Inigo 67, 69, 107, 111, 155
Jones, Paul 143
Jonzen, Karin 55
Joubert 143

K

Kent, William 83, 101, 111
Killigrew, Thomas 55
Kingsley, Charles 149

L

Ladbroke, James Weller 79
Lamb, Charles 93
Landseer, Sir Edwin 89
Langtry, Lily 145
Lasdun, Sir Denys 113
Le Corbusier, Charles 41
Le Nôtre 155
Leoni, Giacomo 143
Lewis, Rosa 85
Lind, Jenny 141
Lindsey, Earl of 153
Lloyd George, David 151
Louise, Princess 101
Lubetkin 41
Lutyens, Sir Edward Landseer
    71, 73, 77, 89, 111, 115

M N

Mackmurdo, A. H. 137
Macneice, Louis 43
Manny, Sir Walter de 53
Mansfield, Katherine 45
Marlborough, Sarah, Duchess of 107
Marlborough, Duke of 63
Marshall Mackenzie, A. 69
Marx, Karl 47, 65
Mary, Queen 155
Matcham, Frank 63
Matilda, Queen 97, 115
Maufe, Sir Edward 51, 93, 115
Mempes, Mortimer 137
Miles, Sir Bernard 95
Milton, John 55
Moore, George 147
Moore, Henry 95, 127, 143
More, Sir Thomas 149, 153
Morgan, William de 149
Morris, William 49
    & Co 137
Mozart, Wolfgang Amadeus 65
Nash, John 41, 43, 57, 63,
    87, 89, 107, 109, 123, 125
Nelson, Lord 43, 89
Newton, William 69
Nightingale, Florence 87
Northcliffe, Lord 71
Nottingham, Earl of 101

O

Ordish 149
Oyley Carte, Richard d' 91

P

Palmerston, Lord 127
Patton, General 81
Peel, Sir Robert 123
Pennethorne, Sir James 101
Pepys, Samuel 51, 73, 89
Pevsner, Nicholas 41
Phené, Dr 149
Philippa, Queen 97
Phipps, C. J. 87
Piper, John 129
Pitt the Younger, William,
     bronze, Hanover Square 61
Playfair, Sir Nigel 135
Plazotta, Enzo 67
Plowden, Edmund 93
Potter, Beatrix 141
Prime Minister 111
Pugin, Augustus 83, 129

Q

Quant, Mary 145
Queen Mother, Elizabeth the 83

R

Raffles, Sir Thomas Stamford 41
Rahere 53
Raleigh, Sir Walter 77
Ranelagh, Earl of 147
Reed, Carol 143
Rennie, John 103, 113
Repton 87
Richardson, Sir Albert 75
Riley, W. E. 49
Robert-Jones, Ivor 129
Roberts, Henry 99
Rohe, Mies van der 77
Roosevelt, Franklin Delano 81
Roper, Margaret 149
Rossetti, Dante Gabriel 49, 149
Ruskin, John 151
Russell, Bertrand 49
Russell, Francis,
     5th Duke of Bedford, bronze 47
Rysbrack, J. M. 155

S

Saarinen, Eero 81
St Albans, Earl of 109
Sanders, John 145
Sargent, John Singer 151
Savage, James 143
Sayers, Dorothy L. 49
Scarfe, Gerald 151
Scott, Adrian 51
Scott, Sir George Gilbert
     99, 101, 113, 117, 127
Scott, Robert Falcon 149
Sedding, J. D. 137
Sedley, Angelo 61
Seifert, Richard 101
Selfridge, Gordon 59

Seth-Smith, W. H. 121
Seymour, Jane 149
Shaftesbury, Lord 87
Shakespeare, William 71
Shaw, George Bernard 141, 145
Shaw, John 71
Shaw, Norman 85, 117, 129
Shaw, Richard Norman 151
Shelley, Percy Bysshe 105
Shepherd, Edward 59, 105
Sheridan, Richard Brinsley 105
Siddons, Sarah 47
Sim, James 47
Sitwell, Edith 151
Sitwell, Osbert 149
Sloane, Sir Hans 47
Smirke, Sir Robert 87, 91
Smithson, A. & P. 107
Smollett, Tobias 149
Snow, William 99
Snowden, Lord 41
Soane, Sir John 69, 77
Spence, Sir Basil 55, 119
Sprague, W. G. R. 69, 79, 91
Steer, Philip Wilson 153
Stevens & Munt 119
Stoker, Bram 145
Stokes, Leonard 143
Street, G. E. 69
Strype, John 47
Stuart, James 'Athenian' 155
Sutton, Thomas 53
Swinburne, Henry 49 149

T

Tanner, Sir Henry 63
Taylor, George Ledwall 45
Tecton 41
Telford, Thomas 115
Terry, Ellen 79, 149
Thorneycroft, Sir William Hamo 69
Thornhill, Sir James 155
Thornycroft, Thomas 129
Toovey, J. W. 41
Tripe 147
Turner, J. M. W. 153, 155
Twain, Mark 145
Tweed, John 153
Tyler, Wat 99

V

Vanbrugh, Sir John 155
Vardy, John 107
Verity, Thomas 87
Victoria, Queen 53, 125
     statue, Kensington Palace 101
     bust, Regent's Park 41
Vulliamy, Lewis 71, 85, 103

W

Wakeham 147
Wales, Prince of
     (Prince Regent; George IV) 63, 109

Wallace, Edgar 93
Walpole, Horace 147
Walton, William 151
Ware, Samuel 85
Waterhouse, Alfred and Paul 51, 59, 133
Webb, Sir Aston 53, 109, 117, 125, 133
Webb, John 155
Weidenfeld, Lord 151
Wellington, Duke of 103, 145
    statue, Hyde Park Corner 103
Westmacott, Sir Richard 47, 109
Westminster, Duke of 81
Whistler, James Abbot 151, 153
Whittington, Dick 97
Whyte, John 79
Wilde, Oscar 149, 151
Wilkins, William 87
William I 95, 115
William III 101, 145
    bronze, Kensington Gardens 101
William IV 99
Willson, Anthony Beckles 115
Wilson, Edmund 45
Wolfe-Barry, Sir John 115
Wood, Francis Derwent 103
Woodhouse, P. G. 105
Woolf, Leonard 49
Woolf, Virginia 49
Worthington, Sir Herbert 71
Wren, Sir Christopher 55, 69, 73, 75, 77, 93,
    95, 97, 99, 101, 107, 129, 145, 147, 155
Wriothesley, Thomas 55
Wyatt, Benjamin 69, 103, 107, 109
Wynne 115, 149

Y

Yevele, Henry 53
York, Duchess of 59
York, Duke of 107, 109

Z

Zinzendorf, Count 153

STREET NAMES

A

Abchurch Lane 98
Abingdon Street 128
Achilles Way 103
Adam Street 89
Adam's Row 81
Adelaide Street 88
Agar Street 88
Albemarle Street 84
Albert Bridge 149
Albion Place 52
Aldermanbury 75
Aldermanbury Square 55

Aldersgate Street 54, 74
Aldford Street 80-1
Aldwych 68-9, 90
Allington Street 138
Allsop Place 42
Alpha Place 149
Ambrosden Avenue 139
Amen Court 72-3
Andrew Borde Street 65
Angel Street 74
Apsley Way 121
Argyll Street 62
Arlington Street 106
Ashley Place 139
Astell Street 142-3
Austin Friars 77
Avery Row 60

B

Baker Street 42
Baldwin's Gardens 50
Balfour Mews 80-1
Barlow Place 83
Bartholomew's Lane 76
Basil Street 118
Basinghall Street 76
Bateman Street 64
Bayswater Road 56
Beak Street 62-3
Bear Gardens 96
Beauchamp Place 131
Bedford Place 47
Bedford Row 48-9
Bedford Square 46
Bedford Street 88
Bedfordbury 88
Beech Street 54
Belgrave Mews 120
Belgrave Mews West 120
Belgrave Square 120-1
Bell Yard 70
Belvedere Road 112
Benjamin Street 52
Bennet's Hill 95
Berkeley Mews 57
Berkeley Square 82-3
Berkeley Street 84
Berwick Street 63, 64
Binney Street 59
Birchin Lane 77
Birdcage Walk, St James's Park 126-7
Bishop's Court 72
Black Friars 72
Blackburne's Mews 80
Blackfriars Bridge 94
Blackfriars Court 94
Blackfriars Lane 94
Blackfriars Underpass 94
Blacklands Terrace 136
Blomfield Road 44-5
Blomfield Villas 44
Bloomsbury Street 46
Boltons, The 140

Bolton Street 83, 105
Bourdon Street 82
Bourne Street 137
Bouverie Street 71
Bow Churchyard 75
Bow Lane 75
Bow Street 67
Bramerton Street 148
Bread Street 74
Bressenden Place 138
Brewer Street 64, 85
Brick Street 104
Bride Lane 72
Bridewell Place 72
Bridge Street 128
Bridgewater Square 54
Britten Street 142-3
Britton Street 52
Broad Court 67
Broad Walk, Hyde Park 80
Broad Walk, The, Kensington Gardens 101
Broad Walk, Regent's Park 41
Broadway 126
Broadwick Street 63, 64
Brompton Road 118, 130-1, 134
Brompton Square 130
Brook Street 60
Brooke Street 50
Brook's Mews
Brownlow Street 49
Bruton Place 82
Bruton Street 83
Bryanston Street 56-7
Buckingham Palace Road 138
Buckingham Street 88-9
Burleigh Street 90
Burlington Gardens 84
Bury Place 47
Bury Street 84
Byward Street 114
Bywater Street 144

C

Cadogan Gardens 136
Cadogan Gate 136
Cadogan Place 136
Cadogan Square 136
Cale Street 142-3
Cambridge Circus 65
Campden Hill Road 77
Cannon Row 128
Cannon Street 74, 97, 98-9
Carey Street 69, 70
Carlisle Place 139
Carlos Place 82
Carlton Gardens 108
Carlton House Terrace 108
Carlyle Square 148
Carmelite Street 93
Carnaby Street 62
Caroline Terrace 137
Carrington Street 104
Carter Lane 73

Carteret Street 126
Carting Lane 90
Castle Baynard Street 95, 96
Catherine Street 90
Catherine Wheel Yard 106
Caversham Street 150
Cecil Court 88
Chancery Lane 50, 70
Chandos Place 88
Chapel Street 122
Charing Cross 88
Charing Cross Road 65, 87, 88
Charles Street 82
Charles II Street 86
Charterhouse Mews 53
Charterhouse Square 53
Charterhouse Street 51, 52-3
Cheapside 74-5
Chelsea Bridge Road 146-7
Chelsea Embankment 146-7, 148-9, 150-1
Chelsea Manor Gardens 142
Chelsea Manor Street 142-3, 149
Cheltenham Terrace 144-5
Chepstow Villas 78
Chester Close 122
Chester Mews 122
Chester Row 137
Chesterfield Gardens 104
Chesterfield Hill 82
Chesterfield Street 104
Cheval Place 131
Cheyne Gardens 149
Cheyne Row 148
Cheyne Walk 148, 150, 152-3
Chiswell Street 55
Christchurch Street 144, 150
Christchurch Terrace 150
Church Court 70
Clarence Terrace 42
Clarges Mews 82
Clarges Street 105
Clement's Lane 99
Cleveland Row 106
Clifford Street 84
Clifton Villas 44
Cliveden Place 137
Cloak Lane 98
Cloth Fair 53
Cockspur Street 87
Coleman Street 76
College Approach 154
College Hill 97
College Street 98
Concert Hall Approach 112
Conduit Street 62, 83
Connaught Square 56
Constitution Hill 122-3
Copthall Avenue 76
Copthall Close 76
Cork Street 84
Cornhill 76-7
Cornwall Terrace 42
Cottage Place 130

Covent Garden 66-7
Coventry Street 86
Cowcross Street 52
Craig's Court 110
Cranbourn Street 87
Creed Lane 73
Cresswell Place 140-1
Cromwell Gardens 133
Cromwell Place 132
Cromwell Road 132-3
Crown Office Row 92
Culford Gardens 136
Culross Street 80
Cumberland Gate 56-7
Curzon Gate 103
Curzon Street 82-3, 103, 104
Cutty Sark Gardens 154

D

D'Arblay Street 63
Dartmouth Street 126
Davies Street 60, 82
Dawson Place 79
Dean Street 64
Dean's Court 73
Dean's Yard 127
Deanery Street 81, 103
Delamere Terrace 44
Denmark Street 65
Dering Street 60
Devereux Court 92
Dial Walk, The 101
Dilke Street 150-1
Distaff Lane 96
Dorset Mews 122
Dorset Rise 72
Dovehouse Street 142
Dover Street 84
Dowgate Hill 98
Down Street 104
Downing Street 110
Drake Street 48
Draycott Avenue 135
Draycott Place 136
Draycott Terrace 136
Drayton Gardens 140-1
Drury Lane 66-7, 68
Duke of Wellington Place 121
Duke of York Street 85
Duke Street, off Oxford Street 58-9
Duke Street St James's 8
Duncannon Street 8
Durnford Street 154

E

Earlham Street 65, 66
East Smithfield 115
Eastcheap 99
Eaton Gate 137
Eaton Lane 138
Eaton Mews North 137
Eaton Place 137
Eaton Square 137

Eaton Terrace 137
Eaton Terrace Mews 137
Ebury Bridge Road 147
Edgware Road 56
Edward Mews 58
Egerton Crescent 134
Egerton Gardens 130, 134
Egerton Terrace 131
Ely Place 51
Elystan Place 143
Elystan Street 143
Embankment Gardens 151
Embankment Place 111
Emerson Street 96
Ennismore Gardens 130
Ennismore Mews 130
Ennismore Street 130
Essex Street 92
Exeter Street 90
Exhibition Road 116-17, 132-3

F

Farm Street 82
Farringdon Road 52
Farringdon Street 52, 72
Fetter Lane 50, 70
Fish Street Hill 99
Fisher Street 48
Fishmongers' Hall Street 98
Fitzmaurice Place 82-3
Fleet Street 70-1, 72
Flood Street 143, 150
Flood Walk 148-9
Floral Street 66
Fore Street 55
Foster Lane 74
Foubert's Place 62
Francis Street 139
Franklin's Row 145
Frederick's Place 76
Friday Street 96
Frith Street 64
Fulham Road 134
Fulwood Place 49
Furnival Street 50, 70

G

Ganton Street 62
Garrick Street 66
Gate Street 68
Gees Court 59
Gerrard Place 65
Gerrard Street 64-5
Gilbert Place 47
Gilbert Street 59
Gillingham Street 138
Gilston Road 140-1
Giltspur Street 52-3, 72
Glasshouse Street 84-5
Glebe Street 148
Glentworth Street 42
Godfrey Street 143
Golden Lane 54-5

Golden Square 62-3, 85
Goldman Street 96
Goodwins Court 88
Gough Square 71
Gower Mews 46
Gower Street 46
Gracechurch Street 99
Grafton Street 83
Graham Terrace 137
Grand Union Canal 40
Granville Place 58
Gray's Inn Road 49, 50
Gray's Inn Square 50
Great Chapel Street 64
Great Cumberland Place 56-7
Great George Street 127, 128
Great James Street 48
Great Marlborough Street 62-3
Great Portland Street 62
Great Pulteney Street 63
Great Queen Street 67
Great Russell Street 47
Great Scotland Yard 110
Great Smith Street 127
Great Swan Alley 76
Great Trinity Lane 97
Great Turnstile 49
Great Winchester Street 77
Great Windmill Street 86
Greek Street 64-5
Green Park 106
Green Street 58
Greenwich Church Street 154
Greenwich Park 155
Gresham Street 74-5, 76
Greville Street 51
Greyfriars Passage 73
Grosvenor Crescent 120-1
Grosvenor Hill 82
Grosvenor Place 121
Grosvenor Square 58-9, 80-1
Grosvenor Square Gardens 81
Grosvenor Street 60, 82
Guildhall Yard 75
Gutter Lane 74

H

Half Moon Street 104-5
Halkin Street 120-1
Hamilton Place 103
Hanover Square 61
Hanover Street 62
Hans Crescent 118
Harley Gardens 141
Harriet Street 119
Harriet Walk 119
Harrow Road 44-5
Harewood Place 61
Hatton Garden 50-1
Hatton Wall 50
Haunch of Venison Yard 60
Hay Hill 83
Haymarket 86

Hay's Mews
Henrietta Place 60
Henrietta Street 88
Hertford Street 104
High Holborn 48-9, 50
Hill Street 81
Holbein Place 137
Holborn 50-1
Holborn Circus 51
Holborn Viaduct 51, 52, 72
Holles Street 61
Hopton Street 94
Horse Guards Parade 109
Houghton Street 68
Horbury Crescent 78
Horseguards Avenue 110-11
Houses of Parliament
   Chancellor's Court 128
   Commons' Court 128
   Peers' Court 128
   Royal Court 128
   Speaker's Court 128
   Star Chamber Court 128
   State Officers' Court 128
Howley Place 45
Hudson's Place 138
Huggin Hill 96
Hungerford Bridge 110

I

Inner Circle, Regent's Park 42-3
Ironmonger Lane 76
Ixworth Place 134, 142

J

James Street 59, 66
Jermyn Street 84-5, 86
John Prince's Street 61
John Street 49
John Adam Street 88
John Carpenter Street 94
Jubilee Place 143
Justice Walk 148

K

Kean Street 68
Kemble Street 68
Kensington Church Street 78, 100
Kensington Gore 116
Kensington High Street 100
Kensington Palace Gardens 100
Kensington Park Road 78
Kensington Road 101, 116-17
Keppel Street 46
King Street, Covent Garden 66
King Street, St James's 107
King Street, St Paul's 75
King Charles Street 127, 128
King Edward Street 74
King William Street 98-9
King William Walk 154
Kings Bench Walk 92
King's Road 136, 142-3, 144, 148

Kings Scholars Passage 139
Kingly Street 62
Kingsway 68
Kinnerton Street 120
Kirby Street 51
Knightsbridge 118, 120
Knightsbridge Green 118

L

Ladbroke Road 78
Ladbroke Square 78
Ladbroke Terrace 78
Lamb's Conduit Passage 48
Lamb's Conduit Street 48
Lambeth Hill 96
Lancelot Place 118
Lansdowne Row 83
Lawrence Street 148
Leather Lane 50
Lees Place 58
Leicester Place 87
Leicester Square 86-7
Leicester Street 86
Lexington Street 63
Lincoln's Inn Fields 68-9
Linden Gardens 79
Lindsey Street 53
Lisle Street 86
Little Boltons, The 140
Little Britain 53, 54
Little Chester Street 122
Little College Lane 98
Little Essex Street 92
Little George Street 128
Little Newport Street 65
Little St James Street 106
Little Sanctuary 128
Lombard Street 76-7, 99
London Bridge 98-9
London Wall 54-5
Long Acre 66
Long Lane 53, 54
Lothbury 76
Lots Road 152
Love Lane 75
Lover's Walk, Hyde Park 80
Lower Grosvenor Place 138
Lower Sloane Street 136
Lower Thames Street 99
Lowndes Square 119
Lowndes Street 119
Lucan Place 134
Ludgate Circus 72
Ludgate Hill 72-3
Ludgate Square 73

M

Maddox Street 62
Maida Avenue 44-5
Maiden Lane 88-9
Makins Street 135
Malet Street 46
Manresa Road 142

Mansell Street 115
Mansion House Place 76
Marble Arch 56-7
Margaretta Terrace 148
Marlborough Road 107
Market Mews 104
Markham Square 144
Markham Street 143
Marshall Street 62-3
Marylebone Lane 60
Marylebone Road 42-3
Matthew Parker Street 127
Mayfair Place 83
Melcombe Street 42
Mepham Street 113
Mercer Street 66
Middle Temple Lane 92
Milborne Grove 141
Milk Street 75
Mill Street 62
Monmouth Street 66
Montague Place 46
Montague Street 47
Montpelier Mews 131
Montpelier Place 131
Montpelier Street 131
Montpelier Walk 130
Monument Street 98
Moorgate 76
Moor Street 65
Morpeth Terrace 139
Mossop Street 135
Motcomb Street 120
Mount Row 82
Mount Street 80-1

N

Neal Street 66
Nelson Road 154
Nevada Street 154
New Bond Street 61, 84
New Bridge Street 72, 94
New Change 74
New Fetter Lane 51, 71
New Quebec Street 57
New Square 69, 70
New Street Square 71
Newgate Street 72-3, 74
Noble Street 74
Noel Street 63
North Audley Street 58
North Carriage Drive, Hyde Park 56
North Terrace 130
Northumberland Avenue 88, 110-11
Northumberland Street 88
Norwich Street 70
Notting Hill Gate 78-9
Nottingham Place 43

O

Oakley Gardens 149
Oakley Street 142, 148-9
Old Bailey 72

Old Bond Street 84
Old Broad Street 77
Old Brompton Road 140-1
Old Burlington Street 84
Old Church Street 148
Old Compton Street 64-5
Old Court Place 100
Old Jewry 76
Old Park Lane 103
Old Quebec Street 57
Old Queen Street 126-7
Old Square 70
Orange Street 87
Orchard Street 58
Ormonde Gate 144-5
Outer Circle, Regent's Park 40-1, 42-3
Ovington Gardens 131
Oxendon Street 86
Oxford Circus 62
Oxford Street 57, 58-9, 60-1, 62-3, 64

P

Palace Avenue 101
Palace Green 100
Palace Street 139
Pall Mall 86-7, 107, 108
Pall Mall East 87
Panton Street 86
Park Lane 57, 80, 102-3
Park Place Villas 45
Park Street, 58, 80
Parker Street 67
Parliament Square 128
Parliament Street 128
Paternoster Square 73
Pavilion Road 118, 136
Pelham Crescent 134
Pelham Street 134
Pemberton Row 71
Pembridge Crescent 78
Pembridge Gardens 79
Pembridge Place 79
Pembridge Road 78-9
Pembridge Square 79
Pembridge Villas 79
Petty France 126
Phené Street 148-9
Phoenix Street 65
Piccadilly 84-5, 86, 103, 104-5, 106
Piccadilly Circus 86
Poland Street 62-3
Pond Place 134, 142
Portman Square 58
Portman Street 58
Portobello Road 78
Portpool Lane 50
Portsmouth Street 68
Portugal Street 69
Prince Albert Road 40-1
Prince Consort Road 116
Princes Gardens 117
Princes Gate 116
Princes Street 61, 76

Priory Walk 140-1
Procter Street 48
Pudding Lane 99
Puddle Dock 94

Q

Quebec Mews 57
Queen Anne's Gate 126
Queen Street 75, 82, 97, 104
Queen Street Place 97
Queen Victoria Street 75, 76, 94-5, 96-7
Queenhithe 96
Queen's Walk 106

R

Radnor Walk 144
Ralston Street 144
Ramillies Place 62
Randolph Road 44-5
Redburn Street 150
Redesdale Street 144
Reeves Mews 80
Regent Street 62, 84-5, 86
Regent's Canal 40
Remnant Street 68
Rex Place 80
Richmond Terrace 110
Robert Street 89
Roland Gardens 141
Romilly Street 64
Romney Road 154-5
Rosary Gardens 140
Rotten Row 102
Royal Avenue 144
Royal Exchange Buildings 77
Royal Hospital Road 144-5, 146, 150
Rupert Street 64
Russell Square 46-7
Russell Street 67, 68
Rutland Gate 130
Ryder Street 106
Ryebrack Street 118

S

Sackville Street 84-5
Saffron Hill 51
St Alphage Garden 55
St Andrew Street 51, 71
St Anselm's Place 60
St Bride Street 72
St Christopher's Place 59
St Cross Street 51
St George Street 61
St George's Gardens 81
St Giles Circus 65
St Giles High Street 66
St James's Park 125, 126
St James's Place 106
St James's Square 85, 86, 108
St James's Street 84, 106
St John Street 52
St Katharine's Way 115
St Leonard's Terrace 144

St Luke's Street 142
St Margaret Street 128
St Martin's Lane 88
St Martin's Le Grand 74
St Martin's Place 88
St Martin's Street 87
St Paul's Church Yard 73, 74
Salisbury Court 72
Savile Row 84
Savoy Hill 90
Savoy Place 89, 90
Savoy Street 90
Scotland Place 110
Seacoal Lane 72
Sedley Place 60
Serle Street 69
Serpentine Road 102
Seven Dials 66
Seville Street 119
Seymour Place 56
Seymour Street 56-7
Shaftesbury Avenue 64-5, 66, 86
Shawfield Street 143
Shelton Street 66
Shepherd Market 104
Shepherd Street 104
Sheraton Street 64
Shoe Lane 71
Silk Street 55
Sloane Avenue 135
Sloane Gardens 136-7
Sloane Square 136
Sloane Street 118-19, 136
Sloane Terrace 136
Smith Street 144
Smithfield Street 52
Snow Hill 52, 72
Soho Square 64
South Audley Street 80-1, 103
South Bank 112
South Carriage Drive, Hyde Park 102, 118-19
South Carriage Road 116-17
South Molton Lane 60
South Molton Street 60
South Street 80-1
Southampton Buildings 50
Southwark Bridge 97
Spring Gardens 110
Stable Yard Road 106
Stafford Street 84
Stag Place 138-9
Stanhope Place 56
Stanhope Row 104
Staple Inn Buildings 50
Stew Lane 96
Stockwell Street 154
Stonecutter Street 72
Storey's Gate 127
Straightsmouth Street 154
Strand 69, 70, 88-9, 90-1
Strand Lane 91
Stratford Place 60
Stratton Street 83, 105

Suffolk Place 86
Suffolk Street 86-7
Sugar Loaf Court 97
Surrey Street 91
Sutton Row 64
Swallow Street 84-5
Swan Lane 98
Swan Walk 150
Sydney Street 142
Symons Street 136

T

Tavistock Street 67, 68, 90
Tedworth Square 144
Temple Avenue 93
Temple Place 91-2
Temple Stair 113
Tennison Way 113
Tenterden Street 60
Terminus Place 138
Theobald's Road 48-9
The Mall 106-7, 108-9
Threadneedle Street 76-7
Three Kings Yard 60
Throgmorton Avenue 77
Throgmorton Street 76-7
Thurloe Place 130, 133
Thurloe Square 133, 134
Thurloe Street 132-3
Tite Street 150-1
Tokenhouse Yard 76
Tothill Street 126-7
Tottenham Court Road 64
Tower Bridge Approach 115
Tower Hill 114
Trafalgar Square 87, 88
Tregunter Road 140
Trevor Square 118, 131
Tudor Street 93
Turnagain Lane 72
Turnmill Street 52

U

Upper Brook Street 80
Upper Cheyne Row 148
Upper Ground 113
Upper Grosvenor Street 80
Upper St Martin's Lane 66
Upper Thames Street 94-5, 96-7, 98
Uxbridge Street 78

V

Vauxhall Bridge Road 138
Victoria Embankment 89, 90-1,
    92-3, 94, 110-11, 128
Victoria Square 138
Victoria Street 126-7, 138-9

W

Walbrook 76
Walpole Street 144-5
Walton Street 134-5
Wardour Street 63, 64, 86

Warwick Avenue 44
Warwick Court 49
Warwick Crescent 44
Warwick Lane 73
Warwick Place 44
Warwick Row 138
Warwick Street 84-5
Watergate 94
Watergate Walk 89
Waterloo Bridge 90, 112
Waterloo Gardens 108
Waterloo Place 108
Waterloo Road 112-13
Watling Street 74
Waverton Street 82
Weighhouse Street 59
Welbeck Street 60
Wellington Square 144
Wellington Street 67, 90
West Halkin Street 120
West Road 145, 151
West Smithfield 52-3
Westbourne Terrace Road 44
Westminster Bridge 129
Westway 44-5
Whitcomb Street 86-7
White Lion Hill 94-5
Whitecross Street 55
Whitefriars Street 71
Whitehall 110
Whitehall Court 110

Whitehall Gardens 110
Whitehall Place 110
White Horse Street 104
Whittaker Street 137
Wigmore Street 58-9
Wilbraham Place 136
William Street 119
William IV Street 88
Williams Mews 119
Wilton Crescent 120
Wilton Mews 122
Wilton Place 120
Wilton Road 138
Wilton Row 120
Wilton Street 60
Wimpole Street 60
Woodstock Street 60
Wood Street 55, 74-5,
Woodfall Street 144
World's End Passage 152

Y

Yeoman's Row 131
York Bridge 43
York Gate 43
York House Place 100
York Terrace West 42-3

Z

Zoological Gardens 40-1